Heritage College and Seminary

"If you have ever struggled with depression or are now, *The Day of Trouble*, written by my dear brother Joey, an experienced pastor and biblical counselor, will help you. The remedies prescribed in this book are rooted in Scripture and will help you grow in the grace of God and with others in your local church. Pick up a copy for yourself if you need it and another for a struggling friend."

Dave Jenkins
Executive Director, Servants of Grace;
Author, *The Word Matters: Defending Biblical Authority Against the Spirit of the Age*

"I'm so grateful for this thoughtful, balanced, holistic, and biblical book on depression. Forged in the fire of personal need, refined by the experience of counseling others, and founded upon the Scriptures, these pages will bring hope and help to many depressed Christians."

David Murray (D.Min, PhD)
Pastor, First Byron Christian Reformed Church;
Author, *Christians Get Depressed Too.*

"Joey Tomlinson brings the warmth of a pastor's heart and the wisdom of a counselor's experience to this helpful book. Unlike some well intentioned but mistaken approaches to treating depression, Joey offers no panaceas—whether medical, psychological, or spiritual. Instead, you will find balanced, holistic, and biblical tools for diagnosis and treatment, as well as a conversation partner who has both faced his own 'day of trouble,' and has firmly grasped the redemptive hope of Christ's grace in the gospel."

Brian G. Hedges
Pastor, Redeemer Church, Niles, MI;
Author of *Christ Formed in You*

"*The Day of Trouble* is a pastoral, practical, and personal treatment of depression. It is personal in that Joey writes as a fellow struggler. It is pastoral in that he writes with wise depth to the struggles of human experience cultivated from pastoral ministry in the trenches with real people. And it is practical in that it is widely applicable to a variety of expressions of the experience of depression. I particularly found his chapter on asking questions in faith to be worth the price of the book. Many will find help in the pages of this book when their day of trouble comes."

Greg Wilson
LPC Supervisor
Soul Care Associates, Flower Mound, TX;
Co-Author, *When Home Hurts*

"It's hard to write a truly helpful book on the serious and complicated topic of depression. *The Day of Trouble*, is many good things; clear, compassionate, concise. But most of all this book is helpful. If you or someone you love struggles with depression, Joey Tomlinson's book will speak your language, give you understanding, and point you to helpful gospel remedies for this dark and common trouble."

Rush Witt
Pastor, Paramount Church, Bexley, OH;
Author, *I Want to Escape: Reaching for Hope When Life is Too Much*;
Certified biblical counselor

"Joey Tomlinson, in his much-needed and timely book, *The Day of Trouble: Depression, Scripture, and the God Who Is Near*, masterfully tackles the issues of mental health and well-being from a Christian and biblical perspective. Speaking with a pastor's heart, Tomlinson helps his readers wrestle with the spiritually, mentally, and physically debilitating scourge of depression. In seeking to help hurting people, Tomlinson draws from years of pastoral ministry as a counsellor, as well as drawing from the Bible, current medical and pharmaceutical studies, and tried-tested-and-true insights from other godly writers, preachers, and pastors both past and present. The result is a book that gives readers a well-grounded, balanced, applicable, and effective dose of biblical wisdom, godly encouragement, and convicting exhortation. This book is extremely helpful for *all* Christians–whether you're managing personal challenges with mental health or helping others in treating theirs. Tomlinson doesn't mince words in his direct and honest dealings with the subject, but his Christ-like love for his readers is evident on every page. *The Day of Trouble* is a well-written, sincere, and highly practical gift to the church, a book that sheds gospel-transforming light on an often overlooked and ignored area of the Christian life. I hope and pray that it is widely read among God's people, for I know it will be a healing balm used by the Triune God to restore Christian joy to the minds and hearts of suffering souls."

Jeremy W. Johnston
Author, *All Things New: Essays on Christianity, culture and the arts*; adjunct professor of rhetoric and literature,

To Brayden

I love you.
Thank you for weathering the stormy seasons with me.

Call upon Me in the day of trouble; I will deliver you, and you shall glorify me. (Ps. 50:15)

If I say, "Surely the darkness shall fall on me," Even the night shall be light about me; Indeed, the darkness shall not hide from You, But the night shines as the day; The darkness and the light are both alike to You. (Ps. 139:11–12)

The Day of Trouble

Depression, Scripture, and the God Who Is Near

JOEY TOMLINSON

The Day of Trouble: Depression, Scripture, and the God Who Is Near
Copyright © Joey Tomlinson 2022

All rights reserved. This book or any portion thereof may not be reproduced or used in any manner whatsoever without the express written permission of the publisher except for the use of brief quotations in a book review.

Unless otherwise statement, all Bible references are in NKJV

Published by: Joshua Press, West Lorne, Ontario
www.JoshuaPress.com

Cover design by Corey Hughes

Paperback ISBN: 978-1-77484-088-7
Ebook ISBN: 978-1-77484-089-4

Contents

Foreword *J. Ryan Davidson*	xi
Introduction	1
Chapter 1 Approaching Depression	5
Chapter 2 Beneath the Symptoms	19
Chapter 3 Voicing the Struggle	45
Chapter 4 Ask Questions in Faith	67
Chapter 5 Combatting Depression Through Corporate Worship	85
Chapter 6 Combatting Depression Through Spiritual Disciplines	99
Chapter 7 Biological Helps	113
The Cure	125
Acknowledgments	131
Scripture Index	133

Foreword

Depression is indeed a challenging reality as we live east of Eden. For many going through depression, all hope seems lost. I remember the many hours I have spent in counseling those battling depression, and for so many, the idea of hope in the midst of that day of trouble seemed so elusive. For others, it seemed as though no one could put into words exactly how they felt. And yet, there are descriptions of similar experiences, even in the pages of the Bible. The Scripture pictures the Christian life as one that will many times include very difficult days. Often, seasons will come in which the term best used is depression. And navigating the troublesome terrain of what seems like a difficult providence can be quite challenging. And this is where I think this helpful book offers a much-needed voice to those situations.

In *The Day of Trouble*, Joey Tomlinson provides a great resource to the Christian battling depression. With pastoral care, thoughtful precision, and biblical clarity, Joey brings light to what is often an experience of great darkness. This work is not put forward as a quick fix, but rather a reflective resource for the long journey. This work comes with many helpful components. First, Joey takes the reader into various biblical texts to consider how the Scripture speaks to those in the midst of depression, but he does so without importing depression into the text. Rather, bringing out what is there in the text, he helps the reader consider the promises of God in the midst of great suffering.

Secondly, this work is balanced in its description of the human person. Recognizing the biblical teaching that we are body and soul, Joey helpfully discusses depression with both body and soul in view. Avoiding the extremes of neglecting either part of what makes us human beings, Joey helpfully guides the reader in balanced, thorough paths.

Thirdly, I look forward to putting this book in the hands of readers because Joey is careful in his discussion of the doctrine of God. With sensitivity to the reader and to what the pages of Scripture teach about God, Joey navigates the intersection of the Christian in the midst of depression without compromising biblical teaching on the doctrine of God. This is often times lacking in many Christian books related to counseling, and I am encouraged to see it done well here. Our experiences, even in the deepest of valleys, do not change the unchanging, omniscient, simple and impassible God.

Lastly, Joey is clear to point out the normal rhythm of the Christian life as one benefitting from the ordinary means of grace. In most works on depression within the Christian community today, discussion of Preaching, Sacraments and Prayer are not likely to take center stage. And yet, in a clear, concise and biblical manner, this work demonstrates the need for those to be central, even while other supplemental means might be helpful for the depressed believer. This is pastoral theology at its finest—keeping the ordinary means in view as extraordinary means are discussed.

This book combines resources from several vantage points. Here, a trained biblical counselor seeks to aid the individual with biblical counsel and pastoral experience. And yet, in addition to this, he provides the rugged honesty of a Christian man who has himself been through the day of trouble called depression. Herein, the reader will not find platitudes, or simple statements far removed from the real experience of depression. Rather, the combination of perspectives this book provides makes it a unique resource for the depressed Christian.

Over a decade ago I waited in a coffee shop to meet a young man unknown to me, who was in ministry. I was working at a counseling center at the time, and one of the staff members there

Foreword

suggested that I meet with this young man—her husband—thinking that we might have some things in common. That first coffee has turned into a decade of friendship, shared ideas, and it also turned into watching him train to be a counselor and begin to offer deep and rich pastoral care to individuals in need within his congregation. That young man, Joey, has become a dear friend, and a trusted resource to offer counsel. In the years ahead, when I need a solid resource to place in the hands of those battling depression, this book will be at the top of the list!

J. Ryan Davidson
Pastor, Grace Baptist Chapel, Hampton, VA;
Author, *Thinking Through Anxiety: A Brief Christian Look* and *Green Pastures: A Primer on the Ordinary Means of Grace.*

Introduction

This book was encouraging for me to think through and write and I am grateful to God for the opportunity to do so. As this book has taken shape, I have been given the chance to think slowly about the subject of depression and thus mine and take as my own those deep treasures the Word of God gives us by his Spirit. And I am comforted greatly because the all sufficient Christ becomes clearer as I spend more time digging—more time mining—more time writing. I find myself saying with the psalmist, "How sweet are your words to my taste, Sweeter than honey to my mouth!" (Ps. 119:103). And I want that feeling to seep into every crevice of my life, especially my emotional life. I write this book not just as a pastor, but also, as a traveler on the long road of depression. And I want you to know that my journey in writing this book has been helpful to me, and I pray you will benefit just as much if not more from reading it.

I've struggled on and off with depression and anxiety for as long as I can remember (although for the longest time I did not have the language to describe it). At some stops along the way I've needed to repent. At other stops I've needed to persevere, flee despair, and trust what I know to be true about God, myself, and the world around me. In many ways, this book is the result of walking through the valley and seeking comfort in the Lord (1 Sam. 30:6). The counsel I give in this book is counsel that I have personally received, struggled with, and shared with others for some time now. As we begin this journey together, I want to help you start with the right expectations. When you read this book, you may find there to be besetting sin in your life that is causing your depression. If that is you, I have encouraging news—you can begin

The Day of Trouble

to be free of your depression today. As you'll see, repentance is the way out, and as you repent and set your mind on things that are above (Col. 3:2) you'll be able to say along with David, "Blessed is he whose transgression is forgiven, whose sin is covered" (Ps. 32:1). There are other causes of depression that we will address too though those waves of sadness may continue to crash over you this side of eternity. And for those that fall into that category, I offer you the words of Jeremiah, the weeping prophet, from Lamentations 3:25–26:

> The LORD *is* good to those who wait for him,
> To the soul *who* seeks him.
> *It is* good that *one* should hope and wait quietly
> For the salvation of the LORD.

For those of you in the trenches of depression for causes other than personal sin, know that the pages to follow do not resemble a traditional self-help book, but rather a resource to help you in *waiting* on the Lord as you struggle. Waiting is difficult for us. We live in an instant gratification society. The things we want are often at our fingertips. But God's ways are not like the ways of the world. In the midst of extreme suffering, Jeremiah had the audacity to say that it is good to hope and wait quietly for the Lord's deliverance. Waiting is worthwhile and I pray you'll see that in our journey together.

Before we begin, allow me to give you the "lay of the land." We will begin our journey in chapter one by highlighting various symptoms of depression. The list of symptoms I've compiled is not just from my own journey but from the experience of those I've counseled, the reports of medical professionals, and from the Bible itself. Additionally, we will acknowledge the debate surrounding the effectiveness of medications to manage some of the symptoms of depression. In chapter two we will go beneath the

Introduction

symptoms of depression by addressing various root causes of depression that include biological issues, changes in life, trauma, and personal sin. Chapter three will help equip us to give voice to our struggle. Oftentimes those of us caught in the fog of depression have a difficult time articulating the struggle. Therefore, we will be mentored by the psalmists as we seek to adopt biblical words to describe our struggle.[1] In chapter four we will learn to ask questions in faith by addressing two primary questions those who wrestle with depression have: "Does God change?" and "Is death my deliverance?" Chapters five and six contain critical spiritual strategies I encourage you to adopt as you combat depression, and they relate to the public and private worship of the Triune God. Chapter seven includes some thoughts on addressing depression by nutrifying the body, exercising, sleeping and includes an extended discussion on factors to consider if you decide to take medication. Then, we will end the book by considering *the day* the final cure for depression will come. My prayer is that this book will be your starting place for hoping (not despairing!) while proactively waiting for the deliverance only God can bring in this life and the next. And as you commit yourself to him, may you realize that you are not alone. Many godly people struggle with depression and creation itself groans for the day when Jesus definitively makes all things new.

---

[1] John Calvin called the psalms, "An Anatomy of all Parts of the Soul". John Calvin, Commentaries of Calvin, various translators and editors, 45 vols. (Edinburgh: Calvin Translation Society, 1846-1851; rep., 22 vols., Grand Rapids, MI: Baker, 1979) [introduction to Commentary on the Book of Psalms].

Chapter 1
Approaching Depression

Depression is difficult to define. On the one hand, symptoms manifest differently in different people, there's no one size fits all when it comes to depression. On the other hand, it's difficult because it can be excruciating and exhausting to describe what's going on in the depths of your soul. How do you bring dark, deep-seated musings to the surface? How can you be that vulnerable? If you do try describing your pain, will it help or hurt? Can you form language around the tears that seem to be so nearby? Are tears justified? Or are you too numb to even cry? Perhaps you're at a loss for how to understand or help yourself. "What's wrong with me?" you wonder and if you don't understand yourself, surely no one else will. You feel in your bones that you are wrestling with something sinister—at least it feels sinister, but you just can't seem to organize words around the struggle.

Being hard to define from the inside and hard to find on the outside is one of the many battles related to depression. Depression doesn't show up on an X-Ray and it can't be detected with an MRI. It isn't something you can point at and say "see, there it is! I told you!" Though its symptoms are present, and its effects are felt to the very core of your being, there is no physical form for depression per se; it cannot be objectively measured. With such a lack of scientific evidence it compounds the problem of articulating the struggle and identifying the symptoms. And perhaps it is even too embarrassing, to simply say, "I'm depressed." Maybe the word "depressed" doesn't even capture the depth of sorrow you feel. Maybe it seems like you are far adrift in a fog of darkness. You are disoriented, unable to see what is ahead, only what's behind. If this describes you, in the words of Aslan, "Courage, dear heart."[2] As we journey in this book, I pray that you are encouraged by the attentiveness and nearness of our good King. And while this side of eternity the darkness may remain to some extent, I know in it you can feel brave and cultivate tangible gospel hope by the nearness and light of Jesus—the one who expels darkness.

Symptoms of Depression
Because this is a *Christian* book on depression, we need to understand that it is a distinctly Christian position to recognize the impact of Adam's fall (Rom. 5:12–21) on our lives. We have a sin nature from birth (Ps. 51:5) and as a result, we commit *actual* sins (Rom. 3:10–12). Because of our sin, we all die (Rom. 5:12), and apart from the intervening work of the Holy Spirit (Ezek. 36:26) in our lives, we will receive the just and righteous punishment of God our sin deserves (Rev. 21:8). Our personal sins, then, can be an accelerator for our depression as well as other's sins against us (and we will discuss this as we journey through this book together). Adam's sin also introduced into this world the thorns and thistles of life (Gen. 3:18)—thus everything worth doing is hard. But Adam's sin also caused a *biological* brokenness in all of us. And this biological brokenness affects us in all kinds of ways, ways which are not a direct result of our personal sins, but rather the result of living in fallen bodies in a fallen world. After Adam and Eve were deceived by the serpent, the Lord said to Adam,

> Cursed is the ground for your sake; in toil you shall eat of it all the days of your life. Both thorns and thistles it shall bring forth for you, and you shall eat the herb of the field. In the sweat of your face you shall eat bread till you return to the ground, for out of it you were taken; for dust you are, and to dust you shall return (Gen. 3:17–19).

---

[2] Aslan's words to Lucy as she and the gang draw near the Dark Island. C.S. Lewis, *The Voyage of the Dawn Treader* (New York: Scholastic 1995)186–187.

Approaching Depression

The earth and our physical bodies have been cursed since the fall. Our bodies are plagued with aches, pains, and diseases and all our labors are met with resistance, even the labor we employ against depression. The curse has made its way around and our body is not off limits. I highlight this passage to say that some of our physical suffering is a result of our personal sin, but some of our physical suffering does *not* stem directly from habitual personal sin—this includes much of our emotional suffering. Not all depression is the result of sinful choices or beliefs. And we need to be slow and cautious in examining the driving factors behind depression (more on this in the next chapter). Furthermore, sometimes depression is more than simply prolonged sadness or grief, occasioned by circumstances of suffering or loss. It seems to me some dear brothers and sisters live with this constant shadow in their lives and they're wrestling with how to process the darkness in a way that honors the Lord. And that may be your struggle, dear reader.

Studies show that 264 million people worldwide live with depression and that includes 15.5 million people in the United States.[3] The American Foundation for Suicide Prevention reports that over 60% of people who commit suicide suffer from Major Depression.[4] I give you those stats not because I think statistics are completely trustworthy, nor because I felt like I needed to in a book on depression, but because when I see that number, I think to myself that all of these people no matter the credibility of those numbers, need Christ. Those people, no matter their various symptoms, need Christ. And the chief aim of this book is to offer Christ to you, no matter where you are on your long battle with depression.

---

[3] Global Burden of Disease Collaborative Network. Global Burden of Disease Study 2017 (GBD 2017) Results. Seattle, United States: Institute for Health Metrics and Evaluation (IHME), 2018.

[4] Their data is taken from the National Center for Health Statistics.

Now, there are several types of depression that have varying symptoms according to Anxiety and Depression Association of America (ADAA). But here is a list of some of the most common symptoms reported:

- Persistent sadness, anxious, or empty mood
- Feelings of hopelessness or pessimism
- Feelings of guilt, worthlessness, helplessness
- Loss of interest in pleasure or hobbies, including sex
- Decreased energy, fatigue, feeling "slowed down"
- Difficulty concentrating, making decisions, or remembering
- Low appetite, weight loss
- Overeating, weight gain
- Insomnia, early waking, or oversleeping
- Thoughts of death, suicide, or suicide attempts
- Restlessness, irritability
- Persistent physical symptoms that do not respond to treatment, such as headaches, or digestive disorders, chest pain, shortness of breath, or heart racing for which no other cause can be diagnosed[5]

Now, not everyone who experiences these symptoms is depressed. For instance, there can be numerous reasons behind weight loss or decreased energy, or insomnia. We need to be slow with labels and diagnoses. But those who are in the trenches of depression can attest and (as this list demonstrates), a battle with depression can affect almost every aspect of your life. That is why simply saying "I'm depressed" doesn't quite cut it for a depressed person. Perhaps, "I'm sinking into the abyss" is a more accurate descriptor. As a pastor, I've seen first-hand just how paralyzed a depressed person can become if they do not get the help they need.

---

[5] "Depression," Anxiety and Depression Association of America (ADAA) (accessed June 8, 2019, https://adaa.org/understanding-anxiety/depression).

Approaching Depression

I've seen macho-men become a shell of their former selves because they never learned how to address their emotional life. If I were to add to this list, descriptors or phrases that I've heard in my counseling include;

- Being burdened by unconfessed sin
- Disinterested
- Feelings of isolation
- Heavy-heartedness
- Overwhelmed
- Despair
- Downcast
- Downheartedness
- Drained
- Weighty discouragement
- Exhausted
- Restless
- Gloomy
- Feeling of hopelessness
- Melancholy
- Misery
- Numb
- Unmotivated
- Sadness
- Sluggish
- Sorrow
- Unexplained irritability

We can also gather lists of symptoms and phrases from the Scriptures. The Psalms are filled with this kind of language. For example, in Psalm 77, the psalmist Asaph[6] remembers the closeness to God he once felt in the Temple. But now, as he writes the psalm,

---

[6] I will formally introduce you to Asaph in chapter 3.

The Day of Trouble

God seems distant. Certain symptoms come to the surface in Asaph's words:

1. He realizes that his spirit is *overwhelmed* (v. 3). The Hebrew word for overwhelmed is the same word used to describe Job's despair in Job 23. For Asaph, there is this unrelenting grief. He, like Job may turn to the right and left for comfort but finds none. Many people I counsel either have an overarching tone of despair, or they use the actual word despair to describe the torment of their soul. For Job and Asaph, despair was brought by tragic circumstances.

2. Asaph confesses that the Lord *holds his eyelids open*. In other words, he can't even sleep. There is no respite from his suffering even through the night (v. 4). For many people struggling with depression, nighttime is hellish because the emotional torment is sustained by sheer exhaustion.

3. He can't even *speak because he's so troubled* (v. 4). This could even be a physical symptom from the lack of sleep. Maybe Asaph is too tired to even speak to other people. But the point is, there is a difficulty in articulating the suffering. The symptoms are felt to the very core, but the words are difficult, if not impossible to form.

Another psalmist says, "I am restless in my complaint, and moan noisily … my heart is severely pained within me" (Ps. 55:2, 4). Could this mean there is a physical pain in the heart? Many depressed or anxious persons speak of panic attacks. Often panic attacks mimic some of the same symptoms of a heart attack. In fact, one doctor told me, that many people are diagnosed with depression or some panic disorder when they go to the E.R. thinking they were having a heart attack only to find out they were having a panic attack. Perhaps that is the pain of the psalmist brought on by various circumstances. Or maybe the word *heart* being used here describes the psalmist's inner self which ached with dread? Whatever the case, this psalmist moans (murmurs) in agony and inwardly suffers. We will examine more language from the psalmists later, but we need to note for now that the psalmists experienced deep emotional pain.

Can We Manage Our Symptoms with Medication?
We can't speak about symptoms without addressing symptom management. And while, we will address this in more detail later in the book, we should acknowledge from the onset that there is a lot of debate about symptoms, causes, and remedies for depression. Doctors, scholars, pastors, clinicians, theologians, counselors, and everyone in between argue about things such as anti-depressants, chemical imbalances, and their effectiveness.[7] There are a voluminous number of books and articles written about how we should describe the ailments of depression and the remedies that do or do not merit exploration. Resources like this can be well worth reading. For example, there was a book published back in 2012 called *Good Mood, Bad Mood: Help and Hope for Depression and Bipolar Disorder* by Charles D. Hodges Jr. In the book, Hodges argues that antidepressants are more of a placebo effect scientifically speaking.[8] Hodges writes as a faithful biblical counselor and Medical Doctor, and in the book expresses a skeptical view of antidepressants and their effectiveness. He also expresses a concern that pills are taking the place of personal responsibility and clouding our view on sin, the sufficiency of Jesus, and the sufficiency of Scripture.[9] I agree with much of what Hodges asserts in regard to the lack of personal responsibility in our Christian culture[10] and I appreciate his appendix on how diseases affect

---

[7] Charles D. Hodges, *Good Mood, Bad Mood: Help and Hope for Depression and Bipolar Disorder* (Wapwallopen, PA: Shepherd Press, 2012) is a fantastic and helpful book that demonstrates a disagreement in the medical field regarding the effectiveness of antidepressants to treat depression. While I do not agree with all of his conclusions, I commend much of his counseling.

[8] Hodges, *Good Mood, Bad Mood*, 49–52.

[9] Hodges, *Good Mood, Bad Mood*, 55–60, 107–127.

[10] Hodges, *Good Mood, Bad Mood*, 96–97.

moods. Furthermore, I have a deep concern about the habits that physicians and psychiatrists have developed in over-diagnosing and pill pushing. I have been personally helped by Dr. Hodges' book and writing ministry. However, I believe the approach in the book unintentionally underemphasizes the impact of the fall on our *bodies*. I understand Hodges pushing against the error of overemphasizing the body in treating depression and I admire his goal, but again, we are made soul *and body*.

With a more open-handed perspective on addressing symptoms of depression from a biological standpoint, Michael R. Emlet, in his book *Descriptions and Prescriptions: A Biblical Perspective on Psychiatric Diagnoses & Medications*, argues that a medication such as an antidepressant "cannot come to market in the United States unless the Food and Drug Administration (FDA) approves it, based upon the results of clinical drug trials."[11] Later Emlet asserts, "More specifically, a study medication has to beat a placebo (a chemically inactive substance or treatment) by a statistically significant margin to be considered effective."[12] In other words there should be evidence that an antidepressant alleviates some symptoms of depression in clinical trials if it has a chance at coming to the market. Yet while that may be the case, we do not know exactly how antidepressants work in our brains (which is rightly a main critique Hodges expresses). It is difficult to measure something we do not fully understand. Emlet brings this very thing up in his assessment of these drugs:

> We do not know exactly how these medications work in humans ... In other words, Zoloft *may* impact the neurotransmitter serotonin in the human brain as it does in basic laboratory research, but we're not certain. Nor are we exactly sure how this might translate to an antidepressant effect,

---

[11] Emlet, *Descriptions and Prescriptions*, 63.
[12] Emlet, *Descriptions and Prescriptions*, 63.

particularly in light of the complex interaction of various neurotransmitter systems within the human brain. This is important. If neuroscientific and psychiatric research acknowledge the current limitations of biomedical hypotheses regarding the origin of psychiatric symptoms, *how much more should we, as those who bring biblical counsel, acknowledge the complex nature of these struggles, taking into account underlying spiritual, biological, relational, situational, and societal-cultural factors.*[13]

Emlet later concludes, "More helpful than a simplistic notion of 'chemical imbalance' is to say that these medications are likely involved with changes in neural networking and neurotransmission in the brain—but this remains unproven at this time. Our knowledge is incomplete."[14] Emlet is honest about what we don't know, but open regarding the potential efficacy of some medications for biological depression. However, the research is far from definitive. Hodges and Emlet agree that the data on anti-depressants is inconclusive. However, Emlet does not seem to believe that inconclusive data is enough to dismiss anti-depressants altogether, especially if they may relieve some suffering as a part of God's common grace for all people. In fact, Emlet's advice is to reserve judgement where there are limitations in understanding.

Richard Baxter (1615–1691), an English puritan, seems to have had an openhanded view of medicine too in light of God's common grace.[15] Baxter frequently treated people for what he labeled as *melancholy*. Out of necessity, Baxter served as both a pastor and lay physician in his town.[16] This placed him in the unique position of treating both the bodies and souls of his parishioners.

---

[13] Emlet, *Descriptions and Prescriptions*, 60–62 (Emphasis Added).

[14] Emlet, *Descriptions and Prescriptions*, 63.

[15] Baxter wrote an entire volume that is, in my opinion, the definitive work for pastoral counseling. It is called *A Christian Directory*.

[16] Richard Baxter, *Depression, Anxiety, and the Christian Life: Practical Wisdom from Richard Baxter*, ed. Michael S. Lundy (Wheaton, IL: Crossway, 2018), 13.

The Day of Trouble

While most contemporary pastors are not trained or equipped to give such comprehensive care, Baxter's insight can be helpful to us. Baxter was thorough in documenting the experiences of people under his care. He wrote that many individuals he treated seemed to be troubled by "physiological disturbances, physical diseases, and general weaknesses."[17] Baxter would describe the soul as perpetually uncomfortable: "[These people] have little self-control in this regard, and though they are God-fearing, have very sound understanding, and are quick witted, they are almost as powerless against emotions such as anger and grief (but especially fear) as might be imagined of anyone."[18] Baxter was not one to excuse an individual for sins such as anger or excessive grief; but even he understood that there were biological factors at work affecting people's emotions. In such cases, Baxter knew that a sharp rebuke to repent of sin would be ineffective because of his patients' state of mind and because it did not precisely acknowledge the root issue of depression in biological cases. In other words, melancholy suffering was complex, and we should be slow as we seek to understand it lest we do more harm than good. Baxter believed that the state of mind must be clear before biblical counsel can be administered.

Now, I am not a medical professional. I'm not even a lay medical professional. However, I try to be a generalist as it relates to my own health care and that of my family. Also I am a pastor, and I have been counseling folks with depression in the local church for many years. I've found that *some* people who struggle with mild to major depression are helped by various biological remedies that help clear the mind. I cannot explain why exactly, but they are helped. And I would counsel pastors, counselors, and members of local churches to resist the temptation to

---

[17] Baxter, *Depression, Anxiety, and the Christian Life*, 114.
[18] Baxter, *Depression, Anxiety, and the Christian Life*, 114–115.

come to broad-brushed and negative conclusions about medications or "chemical imbalances" without all the sufficient evidence we need for such conclusions. Of course, this cuts both ways. We must not speak beyond what we know. We should be humble and mindful of God's common grace in the sciences. And if I can speak to pastors and counselors for a moment, we should counsel with the *whole unique person* in mind. We do not want to approach our care of people as Gnostics seeing the body as a prison the soul is just waiting to escape. We also, shouldn't be materialists, seeing the body as some Darwinian experiment for all sorts of drugs—a sort of chemistry playground if you will. Rather, we are to see the person entrusted to us as someone created body and soul in the image of God and respond accordingly.

Striving with those wrestling with depression and anxiety has been a large part of my ministry. I can say from first-hand experience that some of my counselees who have been on medication are more clear-headed and able to receive biblical counsel better than those who outright refuse any medical or biological intervention. Others needed to come off of medication because of bad side effects. I have counseled godly men and women who aren't struggling with unconfessed habitual sin, but they still can't shake their melancholy disposition in life. Therefore, I directed them toward a nutritionist or a medical professional. After they took the necessary steps, life went from foggy to clear and my counseling with them continued. For others, this did not work, and they are still seeking the best route to manage their symptoms of depression.

Like Baxter, we should acknowledge the graciousness of God in that he has provided various helps for our body and soul as *a* means by which some suffering can be alleviated. Therefore, instead of coming to broad skeptical conclusions too early, Christians should thank God for all the various helps he gives us. God made us body *and* soul. Therefore, we need to give careful and mindful stewardship to both according to the giftings and knowledge and limitations we have.

Conclusion

Depression hits close to home for all of us even if we do not personally struggle with it and the right approach is sound *biblical* engagement. An engagement that acknowledges body *and* soul. That is the purpose of this book. We must continue to mature and see that the biblical worldview is comprehensive with respect to the human condition and therefore speaks to complex and misunderstood subjects like depression. Therefore, the aim in this book is to give you sound holistic *biblical* counsel. I am writing to those struggling with depression. I am writing to pastors with members who struggle. I am writing to counselors. I am writing to friends and family members of the struggling saints. And I want to say this from the start: Yes, the Scriptures can help address depression.

I once saw a drug commercial that reminded me of many of the symptoms I've mentioned in this chapter. The woman in the commercial was obviously depressed. She was sad and alone, while her family and friends were outside enjoying their lives. Then I noticed that she had a wind-up lever on her back and she couldn't reach the lever herself.[19] If the lever could only be turned, she would have momentary energy to take a few steps forward, before winding down again. While the commercial itself was depressing (purposefully so!), it struck me that if this woman could find outside help—perhaps someone who could keep turning the lever for her—then she'd be on her way. The commercial would have you believe medication does this in and of itself. While medication can be helpful to treat symptoms, I would suggest that it is a Person not a medication that turns that lever. That Person is our

---

[19] I believe the commercial was for the drug *Pristiq*—a drug aimed at those struggling with depression.

sufficient Savior, Jesus. And our Lord is gracious, near, and able to help us.

Discuss and Apply
1. Read through the symptom list again and circle those symptoms you've experienced.
2. How often do you notice these symptoms? Which ones are more prominent?
3. Are you struggling openly in your local church? Why or why not?
4. Confess your struggle to someone in your church and ask them to walk with you through your struggle.
5. If you're concerned your depression is biological, seek a medical evaluation from your primary care physician and consider meeting with a qualified nutritionist.

Chapter 2
Beneath the Symptoms

In John Bunyan's classic work, *The Pilgrim's Progress*, a man named Christian journeys from the City of Destruction to the Celestial City. On his way, he encounters danger and various trials. After a fierce battle with Apollyon, the prince of the City of Destruction, Christian enters the Valley of the Shadow of Death. Bunyan says,

> Now at the end of this Valley was another, called the Valley of the Shadow of Death, and Christian needed to go through it because the way to the Celestial City was in the middle of it. Now, this Valley is a very solitary place. The Prophet Jeremiah described it like this: "A wilderness, a land of deserts and of pits, a land of drought, and of the shadow of death, a land that no man (but a Christian) passeth through, and where no man dwelled."[20]

Allow me to interpret this for you: God does not spare Christians from the Valley of the Shadow of Death. In fact, the Valley of the Shadow of Death is a necessity in the Christian experience. God uses it for your eternal good. Yet, the valley feels lonely. The valley is a wilderness. This valley is called the Shadow of Death because it feels like death even as you survive it. Depression can be found in this valley. And once it wraps its cold, clammy hands around you, it's difficult to escape. It becomes difficult to see the Celestial City in the middle of such a desolate place. It is difficult to see how God could possibly use it for your good or why God would ever allow you to experience it. Life becomes foggy and so does the spiritual journey.

---

[20] John Bunyan, *The Pilgrim's Progress* (Nashville, TN: B&H Books, 2017), 80.

The Day of Trouble

From 1953 to 1974 D. Martyn Lloyd-Jones (1899–1981), a physician and pastor gave a series of lectures to the members of the Christian Medical Fellowship, The British Medical Association, and the Royal Commonwealth Society.[21] These lectures are helpful for understanding the complexity of humanity's ailments and can be applied to our discussion on depression. Lloyd-Jones was concerned that medical practitioners weren't treating individual patients by considering their whole person and specific ailments, but rather were applying broad medical practices. He makes this comment, capturing well his lectures on this subject:

> Too many practitioners know more about some details in anatomy or pathology of a person than they do about the person himself. While we may talk more of, and pay lip service to, the concept of "the whole man" and "the complete patient" we must be very careful that in fact and in practice we do not forget him.[22]

As both a physician and pastor, Lloyd-Jones understood better than most of us the concept of "the whole man"—the need to view ourselves as body *and* soul. If Lloyd-Jones was encouraging a mindfulness of each person's temperament, dispositions, physical limitations, and spiritual condition to medical professionals, certainly this should be commended for Christians wrestling with depression and Christians journeying with those struggling with depression. As persons created with a body and soul in the image of God there are numerous reasons why Christians in the Valley of the Shadow of Death wrestle with depression. In this chapter, I am going to focus on four common causes of depression: biological, trauma, changes in life, and personal sin. These four causes of depression welcome Christians in the Valley of the Shadow of

---

[21] After Lloyd-Jones' death, the lectures were published into a book called *Healing and the Scriptures* (Nashville, TN: Thomas Nelson, 1988).

[22] Lloyd-Jones, *Healing and the Scriptures*, 45.

Death and all four causes overlap. No one fits neat and tidy in any of them as you will see through the examples that I give.

Charles Spurgeon on Biological Causes of Depression
Some causes of depression seem to be biological. For depression to be biological, it must be organic in nature. I remember a counseling case which involved a young man close to his 30s. He was a faithful member in our local church and the more I got to know him, the more our friendship in Christ grew. One day I received a text message from him, asking if we could meet at my office. So, we arranged a time to meet and entered into a formal counseling relationship for a while. I was surprised to learn he wrestled with depression as far back as he could remember. As his friend, I never sensed this struggle because he always seemed so upbeat and even optimistic. As he told me of his struggle, he confessed his belief that his depression was a consequence of sin in his life. Because of this belief, we spent a considerable amount of time on personal sin and the nature of the gospel. However, over the course of several sessions, we could not discover unconfessed, hidden sin. We did not discover any ongoing rebellious spirit toward God and his Scriptures. This brother was humble, tender-hearted toward Christ, and suffering in the Valley of the Shadow of Death. Therefore, I recommended he schedule a visit with his medical doctor to explore the possibility of biological depression. After being evaluated by his doctor (a Christian doctor might I add), he was placed on a low dose anti-depressant and within a few months I began to notice a difference in his demeanor and overall outlook on life in our counseling sessions. Does this mean this brother's depression was an issue in his brain? I am not sure, but I do know this dear brother became clear-headed and his sufferings became more manageable *and* he grew in his hopefulness. This new-found clear-headedness made our counseling sessions more productive and less frustrating for him. My friend seemed to have a

The Day of Trouble

biological issue that had spiritual ramifications. For whatever reason, medical intervention wasn't on his radar. He viewed depression solely as a spiritual matter.

There can be different biological causes of depression that must be considered in order to take productive steps toward managing the sufferings of those wrestling in this way. Charles Spurgeon (1834–1892), the "Prince of Preachers" struggled with, studied, and was vocal about various causes of depression during his lifetime.[23] Spurgeon believed that there were several biological causes for depression, and I'll mention some of them here. One biological cause has to do with the mind. Today, experts may use the language "chemical imbalances" when referring to the mystery of the mind.[24] Spurgeon observed that "the mind can descend far lower than the body, for there are bottomless pits. The flesh can bear only a certain number of wounds and no more, but the soul can bleed in ten thousand ways, and die over and over again each hour."[25] From Spurgeon's perspective, the body could only endure so much physical pain before death occurred. However, the mind could die a thousand deaths and continue to be tormented. Spurgeon understood that some people are born this way because of the fall of Adam, not personal sin. Depression stemming from the mind is an unspeakable suffering. Spurgeon said in one of his sermons, "Personally I know that there is nothing on earth that the human frame can suffer to be compared with despondency and prostration of mind."[26] A suffering mind feels hopeless. This hopelessness may stem from how little experts know about how the brain works. As we saw in the last chapter,

---

[23] For the following discussion, I am indebted to William Albert's dissertation on Spurgeon: William B. Albert, "'When the Wind Blows Cold': The Spirituality of Suffering and Depression in the Life and Minsitry of Charles Spurgeon" (PhD diss., The Southern Baptist Theological Seminary, 2015).

[24] Many medical professionals, however, do not like to use this word as it is another example of oversimplifying the complex issue of depression.

[25] Spurgeon, *The Treasury of David*, 3:978.

[26] Spurgeon, *The Metropolitan Tabernacle Pulpit*, 12:301.

even the way anti-depressants interact with our brains is mostly a mystery, despite there being documented positive responses from some people who take them as directed.

Another biological cause of depression can be restlessness. Spurgeon spoke of how his own battle with mental health was related to that very thing. In a letter to his congregation he wrote,

> I write only to send my love, and to assure you [the members of his congregation] that I am greatly profiting by the rest which has been given me. I am weak indeed, but I feel much more myself again. I have learned by experience, that I must go away in November each year, or else I shall be at home ill. If the Lord will help me through the other months of the year, I might rest in November and December with a clear economy of time. I want to do the most possible; and, on looking over the past, this appears to be the wisest way.[27]

Spurgeon learned the value and necessity of rest. We all know that various illness can be worsened by a lack of rest. The same is true for mental illness. Rest however is difficult. It requires humility. It requires time. It requires prioritizing. And a sick person who refuses to rest is a proud person. And if we do not listen to our bodies those of us susceptible to depression will be driven into a deeper and darker cave and we won't be any good to anyone. Spurgeon addressed his mental health by acknowledging his own limitations. I'm sure he got it wrong plenty—we all do. However, he took time away so that he could return healthy and be maximally useful for God's kingdom. Spurgeon was humble in how he sought to manage his depression. We should learn from him.

---

[27] C.H. Spurgeon, *C.H. Spurgeon Autobiography, Volume 2: The Full Harvest 1860-1892* (Carlisle, PA: Banner of Truth Trust, 1973), 404–405.

The Day of Trouble

A couple of years ago, I flew (in an airplane!) to Dubai and met with a church planter our local church is partnering with. Together, he and I attended a conference led by author and ministry trainer, Christopher Ash. In one session, Ash told the story of an article published in a Cambridge newspaper in which a psychiatrist tells of how he prescribes mandatory rest for many of his patients struggling with mental health. In the article the psychiatrist pondered if what he prescribes is "retroactive sabbaths." That story has stuck with me. Ash did not speculate on whether or not this psychiatrist is a Christian. It is interesting however, to see a psychiatrist acknowledge the correlation between rest and mental health.[28] We will talk about the Christian Sabbath in a later chapter, but it is worth mentioning that God told us to rest on it for our good. We should listen.

Spurgeon also believed that an increase in mental exertion could be a catalyst for depression: "All mental work tends to weary and depress, for much study is a weariness of the flesh."[29] Elsewhere Spurgeon says, "I cannot yet call myself free from fits of deep depression, which are the result of brain-weariness; but I am having them less frequently, and therefore I hope they will vanish altogether."[30] This can be the result of long and extended study, or it can come in the form of busy-mindedness or the torments of one of our spiritual enemies, that ancient serpent—the Accuser (Rev. 12:10). An unrelenting mind can be the underlying issue to fits of anxiety many depressed persons say they experience. Spurgeon once said,

> To my great sorrow, last Sunday night I was unable to preach. I had prepared a sermon upon this text, with much

---

[28] I've since been in contact with Ash about that story and he told me you can find it in his book, *Zeal without Burnout* (The Good Book Company, 2016).

[29] Helmut Thielicke, *Encounter With Spurgeon* (Cambridge: Lutterworth Press, 1967), 128.

[30] Spurgeon, *MTP*, 31:121.

Beneath the Symptoms

hope of its usefulness; for I intended it to be a supplement to the morning sermon, which was a doctrinal exposition. The evening sermon was intended to be practical, and to commend the whole subject to the attention of enquiring sinners. I came here feeling quite fit to preach, when an overpowering nervousness oppressed me, and I lost all self-control, and left the pulpit in anguish.[31]

An overpowering nervousness, loss of self-control, and anguish can be a type of panic attack. Many people wrestling with depression also have panic attacks. Often the mind can be sound in the midst of a panic attack, but the body will not reconcile with what the mind knows to be true. I've had panic attacks. When you're having one, you think you're dying. Some medical doctors even speculate that panic attacks can be a delayed biological response to stressful events. I don't see that speculation as outside the realm of possibility. Many people who have experienced trauma physically (say a car accident or a sports-related injury for instance) sometimes do not experience the symptoms of the damage done until years later. The same could certainly be true for mental trauma. Whatever the cause, nervousness or panic attacks are accelerators for depression *and* an extension of them—this is yet another vicious cycle.

Now, it is not lost on me that a perpetual lack of rest and too much mental exertion is also a spiritual issue (again, we are body and soul). I mentioned there would be overlap and this is one of those overlaps. Burn-out, though is real and leads to many physical symptoms. Sometimes when a person is experiencing some of the things discussed in this section it can be because they are (a) burned-out or (b) on the brink of burn-out. Burn-out occurs when we perpetually labor without healthy, humble God-centered

---

[31] Spurgeon, *MTP*, 37:253.

rest and recreations. Burn-out can also occur when we are perpetually violating our conscience. Some of us operate at high-stress (and some stress is normal and to be expected by the way) levels and rarely if ever come down. Spurgeon knew well that we must come down voluntarily, or we will come crashing down. Laboring without rest can breed a "savior complex." When we begin to develop savior habits in the way that we work, we begin to believe the lie that everything rises and falls on *our* shoulders. When that lie begins to play in our head and heart, we begin to feel isolated, hopeless, and trapped. These very feelings escalate depression and can lead to things such as nervousness and panic attacks. If you fear you may be experiencing burn-out, seek out biblical counsel right away.

One final example I'll give you as it relates to biological depression can also fit into the "changes in life" category, but I decided to put it here. Think for a moment of all the changes that come with motherhood. This woman has dreamed of being a mother her whole life. Imagine for a moment—she's the oldest of three and was always so nurturing towards her siblings. Everyone told her she'd be a great mom and she believed that too. Now, she is married to her best friend, and two years later they're expecting a little one. The time has come, and this mom welcomes this gift from God into the home. She can't wait to nurture this little one as she did for her younger siblings. But something unexpected happens. This new mom who has been looking forward to the arrival of her little baby is experiencing thoughts and feelings that do not seem like *her* thoughts and feelings. She's not sleeping, she is having trouble breastfeeding, and the baby is up all night and is colicky. Every other mom seems to have the easiest kid (especially when you check Instagram). But this mom can barely keep up. The house is a mess, she feels like a failure and when she isn't tending to the screaming baby this new mom just sits in silence.

Beneath the Symptoms

Studies show that 1 in 9 moms will experience what is called *postpartum depression*. Those who've experienced postpartum depression have reported the following symptoms:

- Feelings of sadness and hopelessness
- Crying for no apparent reason
- Anxiety
- Moodiness or irritability
- Anger or rage
- Doubt about their ability to care for their baby
- Thoughts of harming the baby or self
- Physical aches and pains
- Loss of appetite
- Lack of sleep/oversleeping
- Difficulty concentrating
- Loss of interest in things that were once enjoyable
- Isolation
- Difficulty bonding with their baby

For many moms these feeling are scary and isolating especially when the sun goes down. And this experience can have an impact on the home that outlasts just the initial stages of motherhood. Do not underestimate the pains of childbirth (Gen. 3:16) and what follows.

This seems a good place to bring back Richard Baxter from Chapter 1. Again, he was open-handed in regard to treating melancholy (depression and the like) with medication. He is known for advising his members to take medications prescribed by skilled physicians as a last step: "If other means do fail, do not neglect medication … do choose a physician who is actually skilled in treating psychiatric disorders and has a good record of curing others."[32] Baxter's counsel is that if the cause of your depression is

---

[32] Baxter, *Depression, Anxiety, and the Christian Life*, 114–115.

not spiritual (or not solely spiritual), you should consider that it may be biological. In cases of biological depression we should entrust ourselves to the care of skilled physicians with good reputations in our community. There is nothing unchristian about taking medication if it is needed. Again, we do not know much about brain chemicals and how antidepressants interact with our brains, but antidepressants have scientifically demonstrated a more positive effect than a placebo in some cases.[33]

Christian Psychologist Edward T. Welch in his book *Blame It on the Brain: Distinguishing Chemical Imbalances, Brain Disorders, and Disobedience* issues a caution to readers not to confuse physical symptoms (emotional numbness, sleep problems, weight changes, fatigue, and problems with concentration) with spiritual symptoms.[34] When we do this, we place ourselves in unnecessary bondage. For the new mom undergoing all the hormonal change in addition to this radical change of life, confusing physical symptoms with spiritual symptoms could be the thing that sends her over the edge. We must be careful. We must not lay blame at the feet of someone who is suffering at no fault of their own. This mindset will only increase the depression, not lessen or address it. So, dear reader, hopefully you see that your biology can be a cause or contributing factor behind your depression. Work with a physician with a good reputation and a trusted biblical counselor as you seek to discern and address your suffering. Very rarely does a person fit into just one category as you can see from this section. Work with some people skilled in the area of depression to help you understand yourself. Even if your depression is biological there is a hopeful path forward.

---

[33] Bruce Arroll et al., "Antidepressants versus Placebo for Depression in Primary Care," *Cochrane Database of Systematic Reviews*, no. 3 (2009).

[34] Edward T. Welch, *Blame It on the Brain?: Distinguishing Chemical Imbalances, Brain Disorders, and Disobedience* (Phillipsburg, NJ: P & R Pub., 1998), 119.

Beneath the Symptoms

Changes in Life
I sat down with a man some time ago who had been in the ministry for 30 years. In our meeting, I asked him to recount for me some of his difficult seasons of ministry. One particular season he shared with me was of his family's move to a church where he would step into his first pastorate. At the time of the move he and his wife had four young children, were married for around eight years, and he was new to pastoral ministry. As he spoke, he told me those were the most difficult and dark years of his life. Husband of eight years, father, new pastor, new state, new local church, new home, new community, and nowhere close to family. This pastor wouldn't know the toll this change in life had taken on his emotional health until a few years later.

He told me that overwhelming feelings of depression and emotional exhaustion hit him like a ton of bricks. It felt like it was out of nowhere. As he told his story I was reminded of those delayed responses I was told we can have to intense stressors. A delayed physical response seemed to be this pastor's experience. He was sprinting in life at a very unsustainable pace, and when he began to slow down, he felt all the change and he couldn't catch his breath. Concerned, his young wife requested he go speak with a counselor, and he obliged. During his counseling sessions he discovered he was on the verge of a mental breakdown and he learned this stemmed from a time in his life where he experienced many changes and pressures all at once. For him all the changes were good, but they were still stressors and he wasn't managing well.

I have also watched people care for a spouse or loved one whose health deteriorated way sooner than expected. As a result, for years, there is constant care and attention given—doctor appointments, maintaining all the house responsibilities, providing for the home, bath time, diaper changes, modifying the house for a more comfortable and conducive living situation all while watching your loved one slowly and painfully decline. This is a form of trauma, but it is a major change in life powerful enough to drive someone into dark seasons of depression.

Several of the psalmists we will look at in later chapters experienced significant change. One notable change was their isolation from the temple—which is to say they were isolated from their community. And for them, it felt like they were isolated from God. This isolation had a tremendous impact on their emotions, so much so they wrote songs of lament about it. They *had* to sing of their anguish. Consider the song in Psalm 42:4–5:

> For I used to go with the multitude;
> I went with them to the house of God,
> With the voice of joy and praise,
> With a multitude that kept a pilgrim feast.
> Why are you cast down, O my soul?
> And why are you disquieted within me?

Again, not to get ahead of myself, but the psalmists in this passage think back to the public worship of God with their community and it depressed them because that was not their present reality at the time they penned this song. Their circumstances changed and it deeply affected them—body and soul. In fact, that word "disquieted" means to make a noise or to be tumultuous. I think of a groaning, sad melody. There was an inner storm going on in the psalmists that had to find its way out because these psalmists longed to be with the people of God, worshipping God. I give these to you as examples of various changes in the lives of real people. And we should not downplay or ignore how change affects our emotional life because change does have a shaping impact on us. It would be foolish to not acknowledge that. We are not stoic and unfeeling. God created us with emotions, and they are manipulated by change. The question is how will we address

Beneath the Symptoms

the changes in life? Because change always comes. Paul learned how to face the changes in his circumstances well. He said:

> Not that I speak in regard to need, for I have learned in whatever state I am, to be content: I know how to be abased, and I know how to abound. Everywhere and in all things I have learned both to be full and to be hungry, both to abound and to suffer need. I can do all things through Christ who strengthens me (Phil. 4:11–13).

Paul learned the secret of contentment in the face of change and even suffering. And that word "content" means deep, abiding satisfaction. The opposite of content is discontent. Discontent means you're unsettled because your *desires* are unsatisfied. This begs the question, "What do you desire?" Paul's desire no matter the circumstance in life was Christ. And this produced in him an abiding satisfaction even in the midst of all the suffering and emotional turmoil he experienced. Paul's strength and contentment was found in Christ his sure and steady anchor and this allowed him to weather life's storms. In fact, even Paul's suffering drove him into deeper intimacy with Jesus (Phil. 3:10). So, believer, don't underestimate the impact a change in life can have on your emotional life. And if it's a change for the worse, it is ok to grieve just as the psalmists did. But face the change with the strength of Christ who is your portion and the object and sustainer of your contentment.

Trauma as a Cause of Depression
Many of us experience depression as a result of sin that is not our own. Whether that be the sin of Adam that brought death and brokenness to God's creation or someone else's sin against us, we all experience different sufferings as a result of living in a fallen world. In Spurgeon's autobiography, he recounts what he called, the *Great Catastrophe*. This was a terrible incident at Music Hall

The Day of Trouble

(where Spurgeon was to preach) and on that particular night a group of people yelled "fire!" during the service. He uses Alexander Fletcher's account to recall the incident:

> As early as five o' clock, thousands of persons were filling up the approaches to the Surrey Gardens. By five minutes after six, the hall was filled to overflow; it is supposed that not fewer than 12,000 persons were present, and many thousands on the outside, and still as many more were unable to gain admittance even to the Gardens. While the service was being conducted in Mr. Spurgeon's usual way, during the second prayer, all of a sudden there were cries simultaneously, doubtless preconcerted, from all parts of the building, of "Fire!" "The galleries are giving way!" "The place is falling!" the effect of which on the audience it is impossible to describe. Many hundreds of persons rushed towards the place of exit, at the risk of their own lives, and sacrificing those of their fellow-creatures ... those who fell through force, or fainting, were trampled under foot, and several lives were lost in the melee ... seven lives have been sacrificed, and serious bodily injury inflicted upon a great number of persons.[35]

It is said that Spurgeon, even 25 years later, experienced bouts of depression from this traumatic event.[36] It can even be argued that Spurgeon experienced what experts today would call Post-Traumatic Stress Disorder (PTSD) as evidenced by his concerns at speaking engagements with large crowds in the years that followed the catastrophe. Many of you reading this have experienced immense trauma at no fault of your own. As a pastor, I have heard

---

[35] C.H. Spurgeon, *C.H. Spurgeon Autobiography: The Early Years, 1834–1859* (Carlisle, PA: The Banner of Truth Trust, 1962), 435.

[36] Spurgeon, *The Early Years*, 450.

about the horrible things people have endured this side of eternity. Regularly I listen to stories from people about terrible losses experienced by them or those close to them.

- The death of a child
- Infertility
- Constant surgeries on a small child once thought healthy
- Child abuse
- Spousal abuse
- Spiritual abuse
- Chronic pain
- The death of a wife who leaves behind 3 small children and a husband at home
- The death of a husband who died in a car accident while making a quick run to the store
- Cancer
- Divorce—a spouse renounces the faith and calls it quits after 15 years of marriage
- Significant Financial loss

These are all actual stories shared with me even in the last couple of years. Maybe one of these experiences hits close to home. Maybe this happened to you several years ago and you're just now grieving about it—a sort of *delayed* grief. Perhaps you've been diagnosed with PTSD. And the people you interact with seem to misunderstand your grief or think you should have moved past it on some vague un-disclosed timetable, but you just can't seem to escape the feelings of depression that your trauma has caused. You just can't escape the darkness.

The prophet Jeremiah experienced depression caused by immense trauma. As Jeremiah witnessed the afflictions of Jerusalem, he expressed his depression with vivid language in Lamentations 3:1–18:

The Day of Trouble

I *am* the man *who* has seen affliction by the rod of His wrath.
He has led me and made *me* walk
In darkness and not *in* light.
Surely He has turned His hand against me
Time and time again throughout the day.
He has aged my flesh and my skin,
And broken my bones.
He has besieged me
And surrounded *me* with bitterness and woe.
He has set me in dark places
Like the dead of long ago.
He has hedged me in so that I cannot get out;
He has made my chain heavy.
Even when I cry and shout,
He shuts out my prayer.
He has blocked my ways with hewn stone;
He has made my paths crooked.
He *has been* to me a bear lying in wait,
Like a lion in ambush.
He has turned aside my ways and torn me in pieces;
He has made me desolate.
He has bent His bow
And set me up as a target for the arrow.
He has caused the arrows of His quiver
To pierce my loins.
I have become the ridicule of all my people—
Their taunting song all the day.
He has filled me with bitterness,
He has made me drink wormwood.
He has also broken my teeth with gravel,
And covered me with ashes.
You have moved my soul far from peace;
I have forgotten prosperity.
And I said, "My strength and my hope
Have perished from the Lord."

Beneath the Symptoms

The cause of Jeremiah's feelings was his eyewitness account and experience of Jerusalem's captivity by the Babylonians. Jeremiah witnessed and experienced unspeakable evils at no fault of his own. As God judged Jerusalem at the hands of the Babylonians, Jeremiah witnessed death, starvation, mothers eating their own children, homelessness and more. Trauma to this magnitude will evoke intense feelings of grief and despair. Lamentations showcases Jeremiah's emotional response to his traumatic experiences and the existence of the book itself teaches us that there is no short-cut to dealing with grief caused by such an event.

We must grieve and as we do, we must not discount or ignore our body's reactions to bad experiences, *even years later*. As time goes on, our memories of certain events may grow dimmer, but our physical reflexes may be just as fresh as the day of our trauma. Some of these reflexes are difficult to weed out. For example, I know people who have been the victim of a grievous sin and crime. Some of these people are numb and by default, distrusting. Life to them seems colorless. They're withdrawn and prefer isolation where the darkness thrives, but where they can be hidden. Darkness and isolation are like old friends ready to welcome the weary souls into further despair. Trust, community, and light have become distant, foreign, and frankly unwelcomed words and concepts. I've also seen people in the church try to introduce good things like community, but for those who've suffered immensely, the pace often seems too fast and abrupt. Maybe this is you. The past trauma of your life is having a direct impact on your present life and you may have become so familiar with these negative feelings and emotions that you're not sure what you'd do or who you'd be without them. You may even be scared of who you'd be without them.

Here me well: your suffering is real and it's evil. Those emotions you're experiencing as a result of trauma are real and some of you reading this book have experienced immense, difficult sufferings far beyond what I have ever experienced. Yet, it is important for you to know that the enemy, that liar the devil wants to use the memory of those sufferings and your present sufferings to keep you where you are—isolated, afraid, paralyzed and depressed. I want to gently suggest, however, that the enemy's attack can serve you instead of destroy you.[37] There is a way that your grief that flows from your suffering can be worshipful and not paralyzing, cynical or embittered (we will talk more about this idea later in the book). And as you grieve, you can say in the company of Paul,

> Who shall separate us from the love of Christ? *Shall* tribulation, or distress, or persecution, or famine, or nakedness, or peril, or sword? As it is written: "For Your sake we are killed all day long; we are accounted as sheep for the slaughter." Yet in all these things we are more than conquerors through him who loved us. For I am persuaded that neither death nor life, nor angels nor principalities nor powers, nor things present nor things to come, nor height nor depth, nor any other created thing, shall be able to separate us from the love of God which is in Christ Jesus our Lord (Rom. 8:35-39).

Dear sufferer, in Christ, you are more than a conqueror. What the enemy wants to use to destroy you, God will use to bring you close and preserve your soul. The Lord has not abandoned you and neither has his church. Psalm 34:18 says, "The Lord is near to the brokenhearted and saves the crushed in spirit." With the authority of the Word on your side, you can say that the Lord is present in the midst of your affliction. The Lord does not turn away from you as you suffer. He does not recoil or flinch. And he is not a

---

[37] We could look to the story of Joseph in Genesis 37-50 for a biblical example of this.

stranger to affliction (Isa. 53:3–12; Heb. 4:15). You are created in the image of God and he can use that which he hates (your sufferings and past trauma) and accomplish what he loves (your justification, sanctification, and glorification for his glory and your spiritual good). Believer, remember you have union with Christ. He never leaves or forsakes you. He is ever-present in the midst of everything and he doesn't close his eyes in fear or runaway. If you are weak, this is good. You are not designed to be strong on your own accord and God does not require that of you. God orchestrated our lives to be strong in the strength of *his* might (Eph. 6:10). Weakness is the way by which Christ rests upon us and shows us that he is our refuge and fortress. Let's meditate on that thought for a moment because it is critical we see God's nearness as soon as possible. Consider Psalm 91:1–2:

> He who dwells in the secret place of the Most High shall abide under the shadow of the Almighty. I will say of the Lord, "He is my refuge and my fortress; my God in him I will trust."

In this Psalm, the psalmist describes the security and protection found in the Lord alone. The psalmist indicates that believers can dwell (lodge or take up residence in) the secret place of the Most High. To be a Christian is to take up residence with God. Some scholars attribute this particular psalm to Moses. If Moses did in fact write this psalm, the phrase "dwell in the secret place of the Most High" becomes even more vivid for us. Prior to the construction of the tabernacle, Moses is said to have dwelt with God in the tent of meeting (Ex. 33). Thus, the tent of meeting was a type of tabernacle. It was here that Moses spoke to God. This tent is where faithful men took up residence (dwelt) with the Lord. In meeting with the Lord, God's people enjoyed fellowship with God and were reminded that he alone is their refuge and fortress. Refuge and fortress are important words for those who've been grievously sinned against. There is a spiritual safety for those who dwell with the Lord. There is an immense peace in knowing that in life's storms, we can hide in the Shadow of the Almighty.

In the New Testament, we see even more clearly God as our refuge and fortress. In 2 Corinthians 12:9 Paul speaks of how the power of Christ rests upon the weak. Paul says, "Therefore, I will boast all the more gladly of my weaknesses, so that the power of Christ may rest upon me" (2 Cor. 12:9 ESV). Now get this—which is my way of saying, "underline this." The same word used by Paul that translates "rest upon me" is the same vocabulary of the tabernacle from the time when God pitched his tent with his people in places like Exodus 33 and Exodus 40:34. It is *also* the same vocabulary John uses when he says of Jesus in John 1:14, "And the Word was made flesh, and dwelt among us, and we beheld his glory, the glory as of the only begotten of the Father, full of grace and truth" (KJV). That means this phrase, "rest upon me" in 2 Corinthians 12:9 means Christ pitches his tent with me. Christ *takes up residence* with me. In other words, Christ tabernacles with his people. Jesus dwells with those who are weak. Jesus is *the* refuge and fortress to those who are suffering and afflicted. There is no need for an actual tent. We are that tent and can dwell with the Lord wherever we are—any time, any place, especially in the midst of our suffering.

Personal Sin as a Cause of Depression
Depression can be caused by trauma you've experienced at no fault of you own, but it can also be caused by personal sin. Personal sins are those sins we have committed. We all have personal sins because we all have a sin nature (Rom. 5). However, many of us have these persistent, habitual sins that increase our depression

by leaps and bounds. This means that depression has a cozy, intimate relationship with habitual personal sin. Personal sin and depression is another vicious cycle. In my counseling I've noticed a direct correlation between some symptoms of depression and unrepentant sins, such as sexual sin, discontentment, unforgiveness, bitterness, or worry. Even though the way out is repentance and joy can be found immediately, many people choose rather to disengage and turn on Netflix. Instead of confessing sins and expressing godly repentance some people quit all spiritual disciplines, succumb to spiritual lethargy, and wrongly view themselves as victims of depression. Here is a shorthand of my advice—stop numbing yourself through fleeting pleasures of entertainment and get to work.

I have noticed that when people lack discipline in spiritual matters, they exhibit discipline in unhealthy, sinful coping mechanisms thus making their situation worse. Some of these unhealthy coping mechanisms come in the form of substance abuse, such as using anti-depressants when they're not needed and drinking excessive amounts of alcohol. Other unhealthy coping mechanisms are co-dependent relationships, Christ-less counseling, unbridled entertainment, and general slothfulness. When people succumb to these types of defense mechanisms they develop a cycle that is difficult to break. In my own counseling experience, I find people on this hamster wheel often give lip service to being sick of their sin and depression, but not sick enough to take Christ-focused steps toward freedom. Another common denominator those in this state of mind have is that they have become unbearable to themselves *and* others. Here is how I've seen the cycle: there is a self-loathing that zaps the vibrancy of once cherished relationships. Almost everything this person does and every relationship they have becomes seemingly transactional. They use their relationships with people to get things from them—whether that be pity or superficial consolation to feel better for a moment. They say they want advice, but they really don't. Often times, their goal is to ease their misery or comfort themselves by chasing temporary highs that release dopamine into the brain. This pursuit for rest and peace without Christ becomes even more complicated and perverse when what released pleasure chemicals (dopamine) the last time fails to deliver the next time. These sinful coping mechanisms develop an annoying tolerance. It is as if they were designed to leave you desperate and miserable so that you'd search elsewhere. The only way out is Christ-centered repentance. Consider David's words in Psalm 32:1–7:

> Blessed *is he whose* transgression *is* forgiven,
> *Whose* sin *is* covered.
> Blessed *is* the man to whom the Lord does not impute iniquity,
> And in whose spirit *there is* no deceit.
> When I kept silent, my bones grew old
> Through my groaning all the day long.
> For day and night Your hand was heavy upon me;
> My vitality was turned into the drought of summer. *Selah*
> I acknowledged my sin to You,
> And my iniquity I have not hidden.
> I said, "I will confess my transgressions to the LORD,"
> And You forgave the iniquity of my sin. *Selah*
> For this cause everyone who is godly shall pray to You
> In a time when You may be found;
> Surely in a flood of great waters
> They shall not come near him.
> You *are* my hiding place;
> You shall preserve me from trouble;
> You shall surround me with songs of deliverance.

In this Psalm, the Lord hinders David's strength in order to disturb his peace (literally depress him) and prime his heart for godly sorrow (2 Cor. 7), confession, and repentance of sin. This Psalm

Beneath the Symptoms

is believed to have been written before the prophet Nathan confronted David, which is *after* David's child with Bathsheba was born (2 Sam.11:27; 12:14). Therefore, it is safe to say some time passed after David had Uriah (Bathsheba's husband) killed and committed adultery with Bathsheba. Now, if you know anything about David, you probably know he was considered a "man after God's own heart" (1 Sam. 13:14). And because David belonged to God, his conscience was too tender to live happily in his unconfessed sinful state. Unconfessed and unrepentant sin in the life of a believer makes one miserable and we shouldn't despise our misery in sin, we should be grateful to God for it. Read again the language David uses in this psalm:

- Bones grew old (v. 3)
- Groaning all day long (v. 3)
- God's heavy hand was upon David (v. 4)
- David's vitality was turned into the drought of summer (v. 4)

Doesn't this sound like some of the symptoms of depression we've discussed already? Again, instead of despising this state, Christians should read passages like this and note the Spirit's work of conviction. Those in Christ will be made depressed to the point of godly repentance. Praise God for the convicting work of the Spirit. Believer, you will remain in your depressed state until you, like David acknowledge your sin and uncover your iniquity (v. 5). Only then will the Lord restore your assurance of faith. Only then will you be able to say in good conscience, "You forgave the iniquity of my sin" (v. 5). Happy is the man whose sins are forgiven. You can be *happy*.

Now would be a good time to examine yourself. Determine whether personal sin is the cause of your depression. Ask someone you trust. Be humble, listen to the answer, and most importantly, *act*. As you wrestle with this section be sure of this: you *do* have sins. These particular sins *can* be related to your depression, and the remedy isn't to view yourself as a victim or to ignore the warning signs. The remedy is repentance and faith. Regenerate hearts repent. You must commit yourself to walk in the light (1 John 1:7). Get out of the darkness. Run as fast as you can toward Jesus. Your transgressions can be forgiven now. Our Triune God is faithful to forgive the iniquity of your sin (1 John 1:9). Repentance/faith really do reconcile you to the one who makes all things new. So, be reconciled, dear friend. Jesus is worthy of your absolute worship and devotion. Being in Christ is your greatest need. I remember when I read *The Pilgrims Progress* for the first time. I wept with gratitude when Bunyan's main character, Christian, finally lost his heavy burden, which represented the burden of sin. Listen to these words from Bunyan:

> Now I saw in my Dream the highway up which Christian was to go. It was fenced on either side with a Wall and that Wall is called Salvation. Burdened Christian ran this way, but not without great difficulty, because of the load on his back. He ran until he came at a place somewhat ascending and upon that place stood a Cross, and a little below in the bottom, a Sepulchre [a tomb]. I saw in my Dream that just as Christian came up to the Cross, his Burden loosed from off his shoulders, and fell off from his back. It began to tumble and continued to tumble until it came to the mouth of the Sepulchre, where it fell in, and I saw it no more. Then was Christian glad and lightsome and said with a merry heart, "He has given me rest by his sorrow, and life by his death."[38]

---

[38] Bunyan, *The Pilgrim's Progress*, 47.

Beneath the Symptoms

If you're a believer, the Lord has rid you of your burden. Maybe your depression stems from you not believing your burden is gone. Believer, your burden is in the empty tomb of Christ. Why would you refuse to believe that? Furthermore, why would you commit yourself to carrying a new burden of sin? You know what it's like to be free. Why would you look to enslave yourself again? We may often silently criticize the Israelites for longing for Egypt after God freed them from slavery (Ex. 16:3), but we do the same thing in our unbelief by pursuing fleeting sinful passions and doubting the freedom our Triune God has provided us. Our Lord and Savior has given you rest by his sorrow, life, death, (Isa. 53:5), resurrection (1 Cor. 15:20), and ascension (Acts 1:6–11). Be released of your burden of sin. Put your trust in Christ. Find rest for your soul (Matt. 11:28–30).

"Know Thyself"
Philosophers like Socrates and Plato frequently wrote about knowing yourself. As introspective as these men were and as helpful as their philosophy may be, one cannot "know thyself" truly apart from knowing the Lord. As Christians, we must examine ourselves in light of Scripture and the God who revealed himself in it. We must agree with the Scriptures about our own condition before we make any progress in understanding various causes of depression. This chapter has focused on four common causes of depression: biological, trauma, changes in life, and personal sin. If you're reading this, the chances are you will find a root cause in these. However, as I said, you probably will not fit neat and tidy into just one of these categories as we've seen in our discussion of them. Take your time examining yourself. Move slowly over the materials in this chapter. Maybe you need to re-read the whole chapter and discuss it with a trusted Christian friend. Whatever you do, do it with a prayerful heart posture toward the God who tabernacles with you.

Discuss and Apply
1. Which of the root causes of depression do you identify with most? Why?
2. Based on possible root causes that relate to you, schedule a meeting with a medical doctor, biblical counselor and/or pastor in your local church to discuss how you can best mitigate the causes.
3. Read Psalm 32 and Lamentations 3. Write the words that describe your current state and discuss them with a trusted Christian friend.
4. Read Exodus 33, Psalm 91, John 1, Romans 8, and 2 Corinthians 12 and spend time in prayer and meditation, reflecting on the nearness of God in Christ Jesus.

Chapter 3
Voicing the Struggle

In the last chapter, we examined various root causes of depression—biological, changes in life, trauma, and personal sin. In this chapter I want to help us adopt a biblical vocabulary around depression so that we can confront it with gospel remedies. Have you ever been startled out of a dream in which you were so scared you couldn't speak? I've had that dream several times and the worst part is being voiceless. It's as if you're so frightened the first thing to go are your words—your very breath. You feel that if you can somehow make a noise the danger would dissipate.

Like being mute in a dream, those wrestling with depression often feel an inability to form language around their struggle, and even if they do form words, they typically aren't helpful or redemptive. For many Christians, there is sorrow and fear underpinning depression, yet silence and struggle are the only things there to meet those terrible feelings. Because helpful, biblical words stay submerged in the deep waters of sorrow, our depressive experiences are not addressed in a godly way. Being voiceless—whether that is actually being unable to speak, or tackling our depression without a mindfulness of God's sufficient Word—is a form of isolation, and depression gains strength in isolation. As the late pastor of Tenth Presbyterian Church and commentator, James Montgomery Boice once said, "A thought, be it good or bad, can be dealt with when it is made articulate."[39] When we can talk about our feelings, they become less overwhelming, less upsetting, and less scary. However, verbalizing depression the right way seems like an impossible task. And it is hard work. It is

---

[39] James Montgomery Boice, *Psalms 107–150 (Expositional Commentary)*, vol. 3 (Ada, MI: Baker Publishing Group, 1998), 640.

agonizing work. It is soul-probing work. Biblically mentioning and subduing depression is a demanding labor, one that requires meditation.

The Scriptures really do give voice to the voiceless. The Scriptures can pull us out of isolation by giving us the gift of right vocabulary. The psalms, as we've seen already, effectively articulate for us our struggle with depression. In this chapter we will, therefore, work through several passages in the psalms in an effort to form language around depression. As we do this, I want to encourage you to read slowly. In the previous paragraph you'll notice the word *meditation*. Meditation is a significant word. Biblical meditation is a necessary spiritual discipline and prerequisite to voicing the struggle of depression. Meditating on Scripture helps you benefit from the vast experiences of the those who've gone before you, especially as you internalize Holy Spirit inspired words. As we study the pain of the psalmists my hope is that you can begin to adopt their language. The words of these ancient believers really can become yours.

Understanding Meditation

Before we can meditate our way through the words of these struggling saints, we need to understand what meditation is. Our culture and especially eastern religions have distorted the concept of meditation, associating it with the practice of emptying one's mind. But biblical meditation is all about filling the mind and heart with the right things, particularly with the truths revealed by God in Scripture. To meditate is to think God's thoughts after him. The Puritan Thomas Watson defined meditation as "the soul's retiring of itself, that by a serious and solemn thinking upon God, the heart may be raised up to heavenly affections."[40] In other words, if we want our hearts to be "raised," we must have "serious

---

[40] Thomas Watson, *Meditation A Christian on the Mount,* ed. Dustin Benge (Peterborough, Ontario: H&E Publishing, 2021), 20.

Voicing the Struggle

and solemn thinking" on the very Word of God. It is no coincidence that the Scripture testifies to itself as being a food to be digested (Ezek. 3; Jer. 15; Rev. 10). It is no coincidence that Jesus tells his disciples to eat his flesh and drink his blood (Jn. 6:51–57). It is normative for Christians to spiritually ingest that which brings us life.

We should all want what Psalm 1 describes as the blessed life. The psalmist here describes this type of life as one who delights in God's law (v. 2) and meditates on it day and night (v. 2). Meditation leads to spiritual health. Meditation promotes the blessed life. Psalm 1:3 says, "He [the one who delights and meditates on the Word of God] shall be like a tree planted by the rivers of water, that brings forth its fruit in its seasons, whose leaf also shall not wither; and whatever he does shall prosper." Those struggling with the drought of depression can still be spiritually prosperous if they commit themselves to meditate on Scripture. If through biblical meditation we are able to continually soak our roots in the Living Water (see John 7:37–39) we can weather the parched, desolate land of depression. In fact, we can weather anything.

Meditation is also a theme of Psalm 119. If you work through this psalm (and I hope you do) you will notice that the psalmist takes great care to note the many spiritual as well as mental health benefits of meditating on the Word (particularly on the Law of the Lord). These benefits include:

- A clear conscience (v. 7)
- Devotion and praise to God (vv. 2, 7)
- Love for and commitment to God's law (the entirety of the chapter)
- Scripture memorization for the purpose of fighting sin and cherishing the Lord (vv. 10–11, 15–16)
- Strength (v. 28)
- Greater love of God (v. 32)
- Understanding (v. 34)

- An increased hatred of idols (v. 37)
- Fear of God (v. 38)
- Boldness (v. 46)
- Hope (v. 49)
- Comfort in affliction (v. 50)
- Contentment (v. 57)
- Healthy inward reflection (v. 59)
- Repentance (vv. 59–60)
- Good judgement and knowledge (v. 66)
- Right view of God (v. 68)
- Perseverance (v. 69)
- Good perspective on suffering (vv. 71–72)
- Agreement with God's purpose and judgements (v. 75)
- Deeper longing for God (v. 81)
- Mindfulness of God's faithfulness (vv. 89–91)
- Spiritual life (v. 93)
- Wisdom (v. 98)
- Self-control (v. 101)
- Hatred for hypocrisy (v. 113)
- A discipline of finding refuge in the Lord (vv. 114, 117)
- Compassion for others (v. 136)
- Nearness of God (v. 151)
- A discipline of going to the Lord for deliverance (v. 153)
- Rejoicing in the midst of suffering (vv. 161–162)
- A commitment to speak of God's word (v. 172)

This is just a fly over pass at the chapter. If these are just *some* of the benefits from a consideration and internalizing of the Scripture, why would believers neglect biblical meditation? Why are believers depriving themselves of this? Our brothers and sisters all throughout history have seen this spiritual discipline as vital to a healthy, vibrant, peaceful walking with God. However, many Christians in today's over medicated hustle and bustle culture are unfamiliar with it. In Romans 12, the Apostle Paul charges Christians in the Roman church not to be "conformed to this world,

Voicing the Struggle

but [to] be transformed by the renewing of your mind, that you may prove what *is* that good and acceptable and perfect will of God (Rom. 12:2). The word of God has the capacity to transform our minds. This may not mean deliverance from all the depressive feelings you have, but it can mean transforming your perspective on your circumstances. God's Word can restore the joy of your salvation (Ps. 51:2). God's Word can make you a productive citizen of God's Kingdom.

Some of the richest writings on biblical meditation come from the Puritans. In contrast to many Christians today, these saints understood biblical meditation to be essential to a healthy emotional life. For them, meditation was a mechanism designed by God to transform their inner lives and keep them from cultivating (by omission) emotional turmoil, despair, and cold expressions of faith. Like the psalmists, Puritans knew meditation, if done rightly, could transform their interior lives and warm their affections for Christ. This approach to meditation produced rich fellowship with God and others and it provided comfort in difficult circumstances. Let us not forget the political and religious climate in which the Puritans were ministering. These faithful Christians faced immense persecution as they sought to reform the church and recover biblical doctrines long neglected and distorted by traditions of men. These Puritans needed the spiritual discipline of meditation, because through it they feasted on Christ and found the stabilizing comfort he offers in the face of suffering. Perhaps the priority and benefit of meditation is reflected well in the writing of Puritan George Swinnock, who defines meditation as "a serious applying [of] the mind to some sacred subject till the affections be warmed and quickened and the resolution heightened and strengthened thereby, against what is evil, and for that which is good."[41]

---

[41] George Swinnock, *The Works of George Swinnock*, vol. 2 (Edinburgh: James Nichol, 1868), 425.

The Day of Trouble

Now, we should conclude a few things about meditation. First, we should see its God-centeredness. Meditating on the Scripture can lift the gaze off one's circumstances and toward the one who is sovereign over those circumstances. Second, meditation calibrates one's love of righteousness and hatred of evil. Third, we should see the comforts God supplies to the one devoted to the practice. Fourth, biblical meditation strengthens the resolve of even the weakest sinner/sufferer. And last, effort is required in this much neglected discipline. Meditation is dependent on faith, humility, patience, focus, and a well-worn Bible. A renewed vision and dedication to the discipline of meditation is what I ask of you as we begin working through several psalms together. What I am going to show you in these passages is only a starting point for what I pray will be a life-long journey in meditating on God's Word. We must seriously apply our minds to the Scriptures, for in doing so, our emotional lives will be transformed, our affections for Christ will be warmed, and his sacred words will become our words. Meditation is a critical balm for us on the journey of struggle with depression.[42]

Lamenting Versus Complaining
It is important to notice that the psalms we are working through in this book are psalms of lament and we must know the difference between lamenting and complaining. We are really good at complaining and really bad at lamenting. Complaining has behind it a godless sense of entitlement; "I deserve/I don't deserve …" When we see complaining in Scripture, we see at its root pride and discontentment. Consider Numbers 11:1:

---

[42] For a more comprehensive look at meditation, check out David W. Saxton, *God's Battle Plan for the Mind: The Puritan Practice of Biblical Meditation* (Grand Rapids, MI: Reformation Heritage Books, 2015).

Voicing the Struggle

> Now *when* the people complained, it displeased the Lord; for the Lord heard *it,* and His anger was aroused. So the fire of the Lord burned among them, and consumed *some* in the outskirts of the camp.

The complaints of the Israelites displeased the Lord. The text says that his anger was kindled, and God judged them. In other words, our God, who is a consuming Fire (Heb. 12:28-29), ate (which is the Hebrew word for consumed) these complainers. This historical account is a good reminder that we are entitled to one thing before our Holy Triune God: his consuming *wrath*. We deserve an eternal hell because of our sin. To complain in the way the Israelites did is to believe we do not deserve hell and that God owes us something. Many of us may subscribe to orthodox confessions of faith, but we are no better than the Israelites on this matter. However, we must remember God is a debtor to no man (Matt. 20:1-16; Rom. 11:35).

Lamenting is different than the complaining we see in Numbers 11:1. Lamenting is holy and is important to God. In fact, it's so important to God that most of the Psalter is composed of laments. Lamenting may have statements that look like complaining at face value (see Ps. 142 for example), but they are complaints of *faith*. Lamenting is complaining in a way that honors the Lord. To lament is to worship. Laments in the psalms are "songs of disorientation."[43] These psalmists would humbly sing their complaints to the Triune God in reverent worship. These songs were composed for what some have called "the dark night of the soul," for times when "weeping may last through the night" (Ps. 30:5). The psalms of disorientation give us permission and show us how to let the tears flow."[44] Tears oriented toward God are a good,

---

[43] Mark David, Futato, *Interpreting the Psalms: An Exegetical Handbook* (Grand Rapids, MI: Kregel Publications, 2007), 150.

[44] Futato, *Interpreting the Psalms*, 150-151.

healing thing. Tears toward God is a gift *from* God. As we lament, we acknowledge that our only hope is in our Sovereign Creator who condescended to us in the person of Jesus and is near to us (Heb. 4:15). It's been said in this book already, but it is worth remembering: "The Lord *is* near to those who have a broken heart, And saves such as have a contrite spirit" (Ps. 34:18). For those of you reading this book my prayer is that you will learn the tone and orientation of lament as you articulate your depression using the words of Scripture. This tone, orientation, and biblical vocabulary will help you worshipfully describe your dark season while helping you remember the Lord is near. He may not *feel* near dear friend, but keep lamenting. He *is* near.

The Voice of Psalm 88
Now that we understand the difference between complaining and lamenting, we are ready to turn to our first psalm— Psalm 88. This psalm is arguably the saddest passage we will consider in this book. It was penned by the Sons of Korah (who I'll introduce to you later). I'd encourage you to have Psalm 88 open next to you as you read this section. In fact, have your Bible open to each Psalm we cover in this chapter. Psalm 88 is a difficult chapter to read, but personally I'm grateful God put it there. One commentator said of this psalm, "This is the darkest, saddest Psalm in all the Psalter. It is one wail of sorrow from beginning to end."[45] I agree. The psalm not only begins with anguish, but it also ends with it. Most laments turn hopeful by the conclusion of the chapter, but this psalm does not and it's unsettling. It stands as a monument to the difficulty and messiness of life in a fallen world. Yes, God is using our sufferings to conform us to Christ's image (Rom 8:28-29), but sometimes we don't see that. Some dear brothers

---

[45] J.J. Stewart Perowne, *Commentary on the Psalms*, vol. 2 (Grand Rapids, MI: Zondervan, 1966), 40.

Voicing the Struggle

and sisters pass from this life in the midst of extreme and prolonged suffering without seeing the other side of it until glory. After acknowledging that the Lord is the God of his salvation (Ps. 88:1) this psalmist spends the rest of the song diving into the abyss of his hopelessness:

> You have laid me in the lowest pit,
> In darkness, in the depths.
> Your wrath lies heavy upon me,
> And You have afflicted me with all Your waves. Selah
> You have put away my acquaintances far from me;
> You have made me an abomination to them;
> I am shut up, and I cannot get out;
> My eye wastes away because of affliction. (Ps. 88:6–9)

> You have caused my beloved and my friend to shun me;
> my companions have become darkness. (Ps. 88:18 ESV)

Isolation is one of the defining themes of this psalm. Consider the poignant and dreaded imagery in verse 18 for example. The psalmist says that *darkness* is his closest companion. Remember, this psalm is penned by a believer, not a pagan. He has declared the Lord to be the God of his salvation (v. 1). Furthermore, the psalm is inspired by the Holy Spirit. And yet, the psalmist felt separated from the Lord and everything good because God was silent. The psalmist dwelt in darkness; in the void of nothingness it seems. Again, read the psalm all the way through, and you will see how the author even credits God himself with this suffering (vv. 6–9, 14–18). Believers are not spared from a struggle with darkness and despair.

Job, for example, was a close companion with darkness. In his suffering, he was emotionally abandoned by his friends and even his wife (Job 2:9). Job's experience is the experience of the psalmist when he cries, "You have put my acquaintances far from me; you have made me an abomination to them" (Ps 88:8). In the startling account of Job's suffering, it is evident God allowed Satan to inflict suffering (including isolation) upon Job (Job 1:11–12; 2:5–6). In this historical account of suffering, we see the intimacy Job shared with the Lord and how his faith was grounded *in* God, not circumstances or good gifts from God. Job, however, did not know what we have the privilege of knowing by reading the entirety of his account. Job wasn't aware of God's cosmic purpose(s) behind his sufferings, even though he declares God's absolute sovereignty and right over all things including his suffering (Job 42:2). Like Job, the psalmist didn't see the purpose behind his suffering (and if you're reading this book, you probably don't either). Job and the psalmist only knew that God was ultimately in control of everything *including* suffering. The knowledge of God's sovereignty didn't alleviate the feeling of isolation. The knowledge of God's sovereignty didn't bring Job's kids back from the dead. Job really did suffer. The psalmist really did suffer. You may really be suffering and perhaps amid your suffering you too feel isolated. You too feel well acquainted with darkness and maybe you're tempted to despair. You may feel that you've reached the depths of the pit where darkness dwells and sorrows abound. There is no place lower you can go. You're at your wits end. And in that place and in the company of Job and the psalmist you must realize that they aren't asking "is God sovereign?" they are asking, "is God *good*?" This question may be your question and it's not a new question. You're not the first person or the last person to ask it. This question is as old as the history of our world.

Spoiler alert: God *is* good, and we see this in what I like to call the hidden hope of Psalm 88. Let's look at this psalm a different way, through the earthly ministry of Jesus. Consider the prophet Isaiah's words regarding our Messiah:

Voicing the Struggle

> He is despised and rejected by men,
> A Man of sorrows and acquainted with grief.
> And we hid, as it were, *our* faces from him;
> He was despised, and we did not esteem him.
> Surely He has borne our griefs
> And carried our sorrows;
> Yet we esteemed him stricken,
> Smitten by God, and afflicted.
> But He *was* wounded for our transgressions,
> *He was* bruised for our iniquities;
> The chastisement for our peace *was* upon him,
> And by His stripes we are healed. (Isa. 53:3–5 NKJV)

Jesus was despised. Jesus was rejected. Jesus had sorrows. Jesus knew grief. Jesus knew *our* grief. Jesus was wrongfully accused. Jesus was smitten and afflicted by God. Jesus was wounded. Jesus was bruised. Jesus was murdered. And leading up to his very crucifixion, Jesus offered prayers and supplications with cries and tears to the Father who could save him from death (Matt. 26:39; Heb. 5:7). However, Jesus went to the cross. He endured being executed like a criminal for the joy set before him (Heb. 12:2). And from the cross he cried, "My God, My God, why have you forsaken me?" (Matt. 27:46).[46]

In Psalm 88 notice the word "wrath" (v. 7). The word *wrath* is commonly used to describe God's righteous anger and judgement for sin. Jesus experienced God's wrath. The Father poured out his wrath for the sins of the elect on Jesus on the cross. God's wrath will be poured out in hell for all eternity on those who aren't in Christ. In light of this we see that this song, this prayer in Psalm

---

[46] Some scholars suggest that Jesus quoting Psalm 22 when he cried out "My God My God why have you forsaken me" and then his final words "Into your hands I commit my Spirit," quoting Psalm 31 were more about him praying and meditating on Scripture. It seems he may have been working through particular psalms. If this is the case, Jesus is not only the ultimate fulfillment of these psalms, but we have a clear demonstration of the spiritually therapeutic benefit of meditation in one's darkest hour.

The Day of Trouble

88; the darkest psalm in Scripture *belongs primarily to Jesus*. The suffering of Jesus is the hidden hope of Psalm 88. The psalmist isn't under the wrath of God. His suffering is so immense it *feels* wrathful, but he is not under wrath. Jesus truly experienced the wrath of God. Maybe this psalm captures how you feel though. Your suffering is unrelenting and raging. Jesus knows your emotions. He experienced these emotions in his humanity during his earthly ministry,[47] and he lamented and obeyed the will of the Father so that we may lament as a people *reconciled to God*.

When we read Psalm 88 with Christ in mind, there is hope. If it weren't for the Man of Sorrows I couldn't keep writing and you shouldn't keep reading. The writer of Psalm 88 *felt* isolated. You *feel* isolated. Jesus experienced isolation. The enemy wants you to feel isolated and abandoned so that you'll continually withdraw into yourself and into your affliction. The acknowledgement of God's sovereignty in Psalm 88 (and certainly Job's admission of God's sovereignty) coupled with the redemptive perseverance of Jesus should lift your thoughts and emotions upward toward God's good, intimate, sanctifying presence in your life. Jesus suffered in a way we will never experience so that we could draw near to God in our sufferings. We serve a God who is involved with us. He is present in our mess—including our depression. He dwelt among us in the incarnation (John 1:14). Jesus became truly man. He experienced weaknesses in his humanity and can sympathize with us (Heb. 4:15). He lived in the shadow of the cross his entire earthly ministry. He knows what it's like to feel abandoned (Matt. 27:46; John 6:60–70; Mark 14:50) yet he suffered and endured (Heb. 13:13). We may feel as if we are under the wrath of God, but friends, Jesus took all of God's wrath for the sake of his people on

---

[47] It is important to note that Jesus was more human than we are. He experienced emotions the way we should experience emotions as Christians. It is our sin that has distorted our emotional life as Christians. As we are conformed more into the image of Jesus, so is our emotional life.

Voicing the Struggle

the cross 2000 plus years ago. This means that God is in the affliction and waves of depression you feel (Ps. 88:7). He is near us even when we feel that our only friend is darkness. There is no place God does not dwell (Ps. 139:7–12). Job understood this. The Psalmist understood it. Jesus *knows* this. He is near to you, dear sufferer, and he is sovereign and *good.*

The Voice of Psalm 77

The chief temple musician, Asaph, wrote Psalm 77. One of his jobs was to lead God's people in singing to God. He was a church leader of sorts. His role was pastoral, and people looked to him for spiritual leadership. In Psalm 77, however, Asaph speaks of crying (literally crying aloud or appealing) to God. A church leader in turmoil—how honest! This psalm details a very dark season in the life of a musical worship leader. These cries are not monotone prayers. These are not silent meditations. Asaph is in anguish, and he cries aloud to God. There is no concern about proper etiquette. There is no concern about what others may think. Asaph knows the Lord can hear him, and he makes his misery and emotions plainly known to God. He doesn't try to hide or cover them up. He's honest. Honesty is good. Honesty is godly. Look at the first two verses of this vivid psalm:

> I cried out to God with my voice—
> To God with my voice;
> And He gave ear to me
> In the day of my trouble I sought the Lord;
> My hand was stretched out in the night without ceasing;
> My soul refused to be comforted. (Ps. 77:1–2)

Notice the repetition of the first verse in Psalm 77. Asaph emphasized that he cried *to* God with his *voice*. He makes his feelings articulate and then he takes those feelings to the Lord. I remember

The Day of Trouble

as a kid being scared of the dark, having bad stomach aches, wrestling with anxiety, etc. At that age those were intense, real, depressive things for me. In those seasons of struggle I didn't remain calm and quiet. Everything was not OK in my world, and I needed my parents to hear of my struggles. *I made my feelings articulate and voiced them to my parents.* I didn't care about the logic of a monster hiding in my closet. I didn't care that I startled my parents out of deep sleep. I needed intervention and didn't care who was inconvenienced. I cried out to those who could hear my sufferings and answer me. My parents ran off the monsters in my closet and they were good at it. They made me feel safe. They comforted me in the midst of my sickness. It is amazing what a warm rag to the forehead and a few kisses can alleviate. The point is, my parents made their nearness known to me. Nearness and comfort are what Asaph was looking for as he cried out to God. In his grief, fear, and depression he voiced his struggle to the Lord. Asaph knew crying out to God was good for his soul. He knew where he needed to run. And he did run. What we need to see is that Asaph's desperation had movement. It was not stagnant or paralyzed. Asaph had hope.

Does voicing your complaints in the form of crying out to God resonate with you? Does it describe what you're already doing? If so, stay the course. Asaph was persistent in his cries to the Lord. His persistence reminds me of the widow in Jesus' parable in Luke 18:1–8. In this parable, Jesus reminds us not to lose heart when we cry out to him. This is something Asaph practiced often. The characters of Jesus' parable are a widow and judge. In the story it becomes clear the judge does not fear God. In comes this nagging widow. The widow of the story is so annoyingly consistent with voicing her complaints to the wicked judge that he actually *grants* her request. Why is this parable relevant in a book on depression? The parable reminds us that the Lord is exceedingly better than an earthly pagan judge. If our Lord is better (and he is) how much

Voicing the Struggle

more will he hear and act on behalf of his people? We aren't annoying to him. he is not hiding from us. He is near to us and is using our depression as a means to develop habits (like crying to him!) to bring us closer to himself.

Friend, the Lord hears you. And the Lord acts according to his good, kind, and unchanging character. His actions (and seeming inaction at times) are magnifying his glory and building you for eternity. Do you trust him? Do you trust him enough to persevere in making your complaints known to him? Asaph's cries to God didn't come from a place of bitterness (remember, these were laments), but of trust. In faith, *speak* to God. It may not feel like it, but he hears you and he does not slumber (Ps. 121:4).

Look at Psalm 77:2. What Asaph is experiencing is described as the *day of trouble*. This "day" Asaph speaks of seems to be a *long-extended period of time*. For him, the sun never set on this day. In other words, Asaph was in this desperate state for a while and he acknowledged the gravity of his (seemingly) never-ending situation. He didn't pretend things were alright. Suffering has a way of slowing down time. Minutes turn to hours, which turn into a keen awareness of seconds. It's like a countdown that never seems to run out, like waiting in slow motion, or like the "watched pot that never boils" or like going to the DMV to renew your driver's license. During these long seasons, all you seem to notice is your trouble. There could be a million wonderful things going on in your life, but your emotions will not acknowledge them. Asaph can sympathize with you.

What can we do in this day of trouble? We wait with hearts oriented toward the Lord. God-centered waiting is not passive. As Christians, we wait as a people who have redemption through the blood of Jesus (Eph. 1:7) and who possess the Holy Spirit who is the guarantee of our inheritance (Eph. 1:14). Therefore, our waiting is hopeful. It isn't wishful thinking, and it doesn't ignore the brokenness of this present life. Christian waiting is shaped by the fact that God in Christ is making all things new (including you) while lamenting our present situation (Rom. 8). This type of eschatological waiting helps you see this isn't all there is. Your fallen perspective and emotions aren't the most important thing about you. There is a grand redemptive story God is weaving in you. There is an ancient song he is singing over you although the song isn't about you primarily. And one day, the wait will be over. More on that later.

The Voice of Psalm 42

Psalms 42 and 43 were originally a single psalm and they open book two of the Psalms. These two psalms were written by the Sons of Korah (who I mentioned earlier in the chapter). The Korahites "were Levites, descended through Kohath, Korah's father (1 Chron. 6:22–48; 9:17–32; 2 Chron. 20:19). They were employed in the performance of the temple music."[48] Hymns have been written using these two psalms to capture the lament originally expressed in them. Now the context of this psalm is important for us before we look at the psalm itself. The psalmists were temple musicians who were far from home and their temple of worship (Ps. 42:1–2, 4). The distance from their community of fellow worshippers and their jobs made them feel as if God himself were distant. Therefore, their longing is to experience the presence of God in the context of their ministry and community. The longer these psalmists experienced distance between themselves and their place of worship the more aware they became of their sadness and trials in life.[49] Furthermore, these sons longed for the days of old (v. 4). If the last few years have taught us anything it is that it's not good to be isolated from each other and our gathering place on

---

[48] Boice, *Psalms 107-150*, 366.

[49] This is not to say that you will not experience sadness and trials if you're connected to your church body. However, experiencing sadness and trials in the presence of God's people is a God-ordained ointment for your sufferings.

Voicing the Struggle

the Lord's Day. Do not underestimate the spiritual significance of the gathering of God's people. These psalmists experienced depression and grief fueled this sad state. Grief due to being isolated from their place of worship and their faith family. Grief because they were prevented from leading the temple assembly in musical worship. Isolation from the gathering that God has ordained and commanded is never good.

I want to note several things in Psalm 42, but I want to frame what the psalmists are experiencing by capitalizing on the imagery of tears these psalmists utilize. Tears give us an outward picture of inner emotion. In this psalm, tears indicate a particular longing—a longing to experience the nearness of God with the community of believers, a longing for deliverance from present circumstances, and a longing for inner turmoil to be quieted. Read slowly these first five verses with the context in mind:

> As the deer pants for the water brooks,
> So pants my soul for You, O God.
> My soul thirsts for God, for the living God.
> When shall I come and appear before God?
> My tears have been my food day and night,
> While they continually say to me,
> "Where is your God?"
> When I remember these things,
> I pour out my soul within me.
> For I used to go with the multitude;
> I went with them to the house of God,
> With the voice of joy and praise,
> With a multitude that kept a pilgrim feast.
> Why are you cast down, O my soul?
> And why are you disquieted within me?
> Hope in God, for I shall yet praise him
> For the help of His countenance. (Ps. 42:1–5)

As I've said, tears are a central illustration here. Tears are real and tangible. Tears speak. What do the tears say? First, these tears imply the obvious; weeping. The psalmists weep and this is good because if words do not form, depression can be articulated through tears.[50] The psalmists cry day and night—which is to say, all the time. They cry so much, that their tears have become their food. Tears for breakfast. Tears for lunch. Tears for dinner. In other words, the sorrow and crying are so frequent there may be a loss of appetite. Now if tears speak, we need to pay attention to their message and the message of Psalm 42 (and 43) is that our souls are lifted by God in the context of the community he has ordained. For the psalmists this was their temple community. For us this is the local church.

The tears are a reminder of the sweet fellowship with God the psalmists experienced in the context of their faith community. When seen in this way, these tears are hopeful. These tears are remembrance. The tears help the psalmists to remember the sweetness of fellowship through public worship. As musical worship leaders, they understood the power of admonishing the other saints with the Word through melody (we see the New Testament picture of this in Eph. 5:19; Col. 3:16). Maybe your tears are reminding you of what you've lost. In one sense these tears indicate tremendous grief, but for some reason you can smile through the tears as you think back, as you remember. Believer, use the past you long for to help you wait patiently and hopefully for the future that is so much better. Or as you think on your past, go even further to the past. Go back to before you were born. Go back 2000 years ago and hear the words of your faithful Savior who invites

---

[50] Remember God created us body and soul. Some research even shows that crying helps soothe emotional pain by releasing oxytocin and endorphins which is why many people feel a weight lifted after crying. For example, see Asmir Gračanin, Lauren M. Bylsma, and Ad J.J.M. Vingerhoets, "Is Crying a Self-Soothing Behavior?" *Frontiers in Psychology* 5 (May 28, 2014).

Voicing the Struggle

you to come to him for the releasing of your burden so that you may find rest (Matt. 11:28–30).

Your tears can be remembrance, but they can also, much like Job's friends, make you feel faithless. We see this in these psalms. The tears ask you accusatorily, "where is your God?" (v. 3). Faithless. Maybe that is a label you've been embracing because that's what your tears seem to be saying to you. This kind of label pushes your head down in defeat as you walk—it affects the very posture of your body. You believe people see the label even as you worship. Job rejected the accusation of faithlessness from his friends as he suffered, and it kept him from despair. Maybe you should reject that label as well. A battle with depression does not dictate the quality or authenticity of your faith. If anything, the thorn of depression can be used as a tool to increase your faith in God much like Paul's thorn reminded him of Christ's all-sufficient grace (2 Cor. 12:9).

Tears also serve as a check engine light. They convince the psalmists that things are not well with their souls. Thus, they begin a much needed dialogue with the soul. The psalmists addressed the inner man with a series of questions and statements (vv. 3, 5). Through these questions and statements, we see these men preaching to their downcast and disquieted souls and in doing so they teach us to do the same. The psalmists use the old stories about their faithful, sovereign Sustainer and the assembly of the saints. These good stories have been diligently passed down from generation to generation. If you read all of Psalm 42 and 43 you know there is repetition; there is no quick fix. The psalmists long to feel pleasure in their worship of the King, but the inner turmoil remains. The tears keep saying, "where is your inner peace?" But the psalmists are committed to respond, "Hope in God, for I shall yet praise him For the help of His countenance" (v. 5).

Maybe you can identify with the Sons of Korah and some of the language they use as they lament: tears as food; tears because of what is lost; tears as evidence of faithlessness; tears as evidence of inner turmoil. If you feel like the psalmists of Psalms 42 and 43 follow them all the way, dear believer! In the midst of their depression, they like Asaph patiently hoped in God. Sometimes all you can do is sit still (a very difficult habit to cultivate). To sit still as a Christian means to trust God, to know he *is* God (Ps. 46:10). The temptation here, though, is to sit still until *we* deem it time to move. But the Lord is in no hurry. He is not frantic and he tells us to be still—to not move a muscle. We are to be *fixed* to him. Our trusting stillness declares him in control of our thoughts, feelings, and emotions. Therefore, the psalmists patiently hoped in God. And in doing so they were reminded that they would again praise the Lord. They trusted the Lord would lift up their countenance, one day. This way of remembering is an anchor in the paralyzing storm of depression. The winds of depression may rage, but the Lord and his grip on us (John 10:28–30) is immovable because he's unchangeable (Mal. 3:6).

Will You Speak?
Dear friend, do you identify with the language of these struggling psalmists? Language like isolation, darkness as a close companion, wrath, a long day of trouble, and tears? For those of us that wrestle with depression these words (and the posture of the psalmists) can be used in a way that allows us to address our depression before God and in God's community. And as we make a habit of articulating and addressing, we will grow in our ability to recall that *these feelings and dispositions are not foreign to the Scriptures. You're not alone.* Keep persevering. Keep turning to the Lord with your depression and remember you have the inspired words of God to help you form language to express how you feel. *Use* this sacred language. Turn these inspired words of God into your own holy laments to him. These prayers can be *your* prayers to the Lord. These songs can be *your* songs. Sift through them and adopt

Voicing the Struggle

them into your vocabulary. The imagery given to us in these psalms develops ways in which we can describe depression to God and other people using the inspired words of Scripture. Once we describe depression biblically, we can address it in a way that honors the Lord using the gospel remedies God has provided us.

Discuss and Apply
1. What is biblical meditation?
2. Are you complaining or lamenting? What is the difference?
3. What in this chapter gives you hope?
4. Establish a consistent prayer life. Begin to use these psalms as an outline for your own personal prayers and laments to God.
5. Be honest about your emotions with a trusted friend. Write down some of the biblical language that best describes how you feel.
6. Develop the daily habit of being still before God. Meditate on each of the psalms covered in this chapter. Find a space to be regularly quiet and patient in an effort to cultivate a trustworthy heart posture toward the Lord.

Chapter 4
Ask Questions in Faith

Kids ask lots of questions and I love how they ask them with "level ten" expectation. Their expectation comes from a trust in the person they're addressing. They believe this person has answers, especially if that person is an adult. Kids just know instinctively deep down in their gut, that adults have every answer to every question they could possibly think of. In case you didn't know, parents are experts in everything. When my kids ask questions, they do so with bated breath. And every question they ask me comes across as the most important question of their lives. They can't wait to hear what my response is going to be, and no matter how I answer, they trust that I'm the authority on the subject at hand. Did you know a lion can absolutely beat a Tyrannosaurs Rex in a boxing or bowling match—little arms remember? When kids ask questions they remind us of Jesus' words in Matthew 18:3 when he said, "Assuredly, I say to you, unless you are converted and become as little children, you will by no means enter the kingdom of heaven." Little children can teach us about asking questions well if only we'd slow down and pay attention. Kids are experts in questions, questions that aren't jaded or cynical questions, but rather genuine. Children can teach us how to ask questions from a place of trust, a place of *faith*.

In the last chapter, we learned the Scriptures are sufficient in helping us form language around our depression. Putting biblical words around our struggle allows us to confront that struggle in a healthy, God honoring way. In this chapter we are going to examine questions addressed to and about God in Scripture. These are questions you may have asked at some point. These questions are almost too uncomfortable to read. Some of you may be surprised to find such questions in Scripture. Can finite, sinful people ask questions about and to the Holy Creator of the Cosmos? At first glance, these questions to God seem irreverent, thoughtless, and even arrogant. But what if a child were asking them? And can we, like children, ask seemingly absurd questions to our Father in heaven? As struggling Christians, we need to see that these questions are ok and even acceptable to God. These questions in Scripture were inspired and preserved by the Holy Spirit. These sacred words were put into the canon of Scripture, and we can use them so long as we have the proper heart posture, like a child. By the end of this chapter, we will see that we really can pray questions like those we see in these psalms, and we can have confidence that the Lord hears us and he answers us according to his will.

Question 1: Does God Change His Love and Posture Toward Me?

> Will the Lord cast off forever?
> And will he be favorable no more?
> Has his mercy ceased forever?
> Has his promise failed forevermore?
> Has God forgotten to be gracious?
> Has he in anger shut up his tender mercies? Selah.
> (Ps. 77:7–9 ESV)

Six questions. Six questions which at the root is asking one central question: does God change his love and posture toward me? If we were to take this passage and make it more conversational it might sound like Eugene Peterson's paraphrase in *The Message*[51]:

---

[51] I am aware of the controversies surrounding Peterson and particularly this paraphrase. I am only using the paraphrase illustratively here. I am not commending it as a translation for Bible reading or preaching. I include it here to help aid you in seeing how appropriate it is for us to ask questions in faith.

Ask Questions in Faith

> Will the Lord walk off and leave us for good?
>   Will he never smile again?
> Is his love worn threadbare?
>   Has his salvation promise burned out?
> Has God forgotten his manners?
>   Has he angrily stalked off and left us?
> "Just my luck," I said. "The High God goes out of business just the moment I need him."
> (Ps. 77:7–10 The Message)

These are real, raw, honest, and uncomfortable questions. Reading Peterson's paraphrase perhaps makes these questions even more disagreeable since it closes the cultural gap for 21st-century readers. Was the Psalmist[52] sinning against God to pose such questions? Are these questions blasphemous? He was not sinning against God and these questions are not blasphemous and I'll tell you why. First, we need to understand that these questions were posed by someone who experienced the power and presence of God. The reason Asaph asked these questions is because he had known experiential closeness with God. God's presence wasn't something Asaph just read or heard about. He had first-hand knowledge. Asaph knew God's favor, believed his promises, trusted his grace, known his mercy, and experienced his compassion. That is why he could ask these seemingly audacious yet acceptable questions relating to those attributes of God. Asaph *knew* the Lord. His questions are *informed* with experience of God's faithfulness and the testimonies of his forefathers regarding God's faithfulness.

Second these are questions asked in the context of a faith community. We discovered in the last chapter that Asaph was a chief temple musician. He led God's people in musical worship. Think of him as a pastor who leads the singing on Sundays. Asaph was

---

[52] This Psalmist is identified as Asaph, the chief Temple musician I introduced you to in the last chapter.

not speaking like an embittered, isolated, self-professed Christian touting the mantra "I don't need the church." Asaph asked his questions as a believer connected to his larger community. In fact, this psalm was written not just as a personal prayer but as a *corporate* prayer. Asaph's questions were to be utilized for lament (remember that word?) by the entire believing community. The questions were not irreverent, hostile, or accusatory. They were warm and worshipful. Asaph was desperate to feel the presence of God in the context of the people of God. And he spoke not just for himself, but also for those he led in worship through song. We are uncomfortable with questions like what we see in Psalm 77 because we aren't well rounded in our worship of the Triune God. The Holy Spirit has given us a vast vocabulary in the Scripture, and we tap into very little of it.

Relate this to where you are in your struggle. We've already established that depression is isolating. When we isolate ourselves and internalize our struggle, we become too focused on self and the depression only grows in its intensity and portending evils. Now stop and hear a few words of counsel about intentionally isolating ourselves because I've seen this habit in those I've counseled with depression: First, isolation is not good. God has ordained the local church as a means by which Christians persevere in the faith (Heb. 3:12–14). Those whose hearts have been captivated by the gospel need to see the value in suffering in the company of fellow brothers and sisters in Christ. Second, your struggle isn't about just you. There is purpose in your suffering. God is using your fight with depression to bring himself glory. He is using your depression to conform you more into the image of Jesus—that is to sanctify you by his Spirit, and he is using your depression to point others toward himself. *How* you struggle communicates weighty, eternal things to a doubt-filled, onlooking world. As you struggle well, you are announcing the Lordship of Jesus over everything

Ask Questions in Faith

including your emotional life. And this announcement encourages those in Christ *and* those you're evangelizing. As you struggle well in community, you are showing those around you how to persevere in the fight. Ultimately, you are saying alongside the author of Hebrews, seek the city to come (Heb. 13:12–13).

So, Asaph asked these questions in faith. Now, there is a central and crucial truth undergirding Asaph's questions that we must see: the *immutability* of God. Asaph knew and confessed the unchangeableness of God. The answer to each question posed by Asaph and his community is a resounding "no." No, God has not abandoned us. However, this begs the question, what of the Scriptures that seem to indicate that God *does* change? How can we be sure God has not left us when there seem to be passages that indicate that he does in fact change? There are Scriptures that speak of God regretting (Gen. 6:6), changing his purpose (Ex. 32:10–14), becoming angry (Num. 11:1), or turning from his anger (Deut. 13:17)? Do these Scriptures indicate that God is changeable and emotional? And if he is, how can we find any comfort in his promises and character? The 17th-century Scottish theologian, Hugh Binning, helps us answer these questions:

> All these changes of his works, all the successions of times, the variation of dealings, the alteration of dispensations in all ages were at once in his mind, and all before him… Not only [does] he not change his mind, but his mind and thought is one, of all, & concerning all: Our poor, narrow and limited minds, must part their thoughts among many businesses, one thought for this, another for that, and one after another: but with him there is neither succession of Counsels and purposes, nor yet plurality, but as with one opening of his eye, he beholds all things as they are.[53]

---

[53] Hugh Binning, *The Works of Hugh Binning* (Oxford, England: Oxford University, 1735), 95.

In other words, what we perceive of as changes in God are not changes in him at all. The Scriptures referenced above speak of changes to *our* circumstances, but they are actions God predetermined to do in eternity past and they are *fixed*. That is to say that Scripture uses the word "regretted" in verses like Genesis 6:6 with a uniquely divine meaning: "And the Lord regretted that he had made man on the earth, and it grieved him to his heart." We should not interpret this use of the word "regretted" as God making a mistake and correcting that mistake. We know God does not make mistakes and has no need of repentance:

> God is not a man, that he should lie,
> Nor a son of man, that he should repent.
> Has He said, and will he not do?
> Or has he spoken, and will he not make it good?
> (Num. 23:19 ESV)

So how are we to understand a passage like Genesis 6:6? In that passage God is using Moses to communicate that something is about to happen. God is about to act. And we know from the context of Genesis 6:6 that God floods the earth. He judges the whole world with a flood. The only people God saves are Noah and his family. In the flood, sinful humankind comes into direct contact with God's wrath. However, this is something God fixed to do *before* the foundation of the world. This isn't God being emotional. This isn't God changing his mind about his creation. God wasn't surprised by the wickedness of the human race and decided to react accordingly. God's anger isn't mutable. God's love isn't mutable. And that is because all that is in God *is* God and God is unchanging. God is without parts or passions.[54] The word "regret"

---

[54] This is a doctrine known as Divine Impassability. It is mentioned in the confession of my local church: the 1689 London Baptist Confession of Faith. Chapter 2 beginning in paragraph 1 says, "The Lord our God is but one only living and true God;

Ask Questions in Faith

in this Genesis passage simply indicates that the Lord is about to execute a judgment that is a change experientially for his creation, but it is the outworking of his fixed eternal decree, based on his immutable character.

Why is this theological and philosophical discussion important to include in a book about depression? The prophet Malachi gives us the answer:

> For I am the Lord, I do not change;
> Therefore, you are not consumed,
> O sons of Jacob.
> (Mal. 3:6)

If the Lord had the capacity to change and his changes were based on *our* ever-changing emotions, we would have no reason to be hopeful in the midst of our depression. If God changes, you should put this book down right now. If Asaph could answer, "yes" to any of his six questions, we would be in a sad, pitiful state. Even if our existence added, changed, or brought out something new in God, we'd be doomed. We'd be doomed because God is changeable. If he is changeable, he is not all knowing. If he is not all knowing he is not perfect. If he is not perfect, then he is a lot like us. If he is a lot like us, then he isn't God. If he isn't God, he isn't worthy of our worship and he has no power to deliver us from our sins and much less our depression. If our depression is the result of God changing his posture toward us, then there really is no promise of his to which we can cling to and trust. There could be no confidence in the gospel, no assurance of salvation,

---

whose subsistence is in and of Himself, infinite in being and perfection; whose essence cannot be comprehended by any but Himself; a most pure spirit, invisible, without body, parts, or passions." For a good primer on this, see Samuel Renihan, *God without Passions: A Practical and Pastoral Study of Divine Impassability* (Palmdale, CA: RBAP, 2015).

The Day of Trouble

and no hope of eternity (Paul uses this sort of logic in 1 Corinthians 15:19). *But* the Scripture reminds us time and time again that God stays the same. God *is*. That is foreign to our fast-paced and ever-changing culture, but it is good and true. God is immutable. He doesn't budge—not a bit and his posture toward us stays the same. Breathe in these Scriptures about the unchanging nature of our Triune God and rest assured that Asaph's questions are grounded in his knowledge of God's unchangeableness:

> Of old You laid the foundation of the earth,
> And the heavens are the work of Your hands.
> They will perish, but You will endure;
> Yes, they will all grow old like a garment;
> Like a cloak You will change them,
> And they will be changed.
> But You are the same,
> And Your years will have no end.
> (Ps. 102:25–27)

> God is not a man, that he should lie, nor a son of man that he should change his mind. Has he said, and will he not do? Or has he spoken, and will he not make it good?
> (Num. 23:19)

> Jesus Christ is the same yesterday, today, and forever.
> (Heb. 13:8)

> Every good gift and every perfect gift is from above, and comes down from the Father of lights, with whom there is no variation or shadow of turning.
> (Ja. 1:17)

Now spend time worshipping your immutable God. You've breathed these Scriptures in deeply now exhale them into prayers to the Lord. Meditate and memorize these passages and use them to inform your emotions—especially your depressive emotions

Ask Questions in Faith

that our unchanging Triune God is faithful to save and *preserve* you. Asaph used questions to remind himself that God is unchanging. Depressed people can often be too focused on self and circumstances. We need a realignment. We need to be God-focused. Asking questions like those of Asaph can be a strategy of remembering what's true about God and therefore what's true about you.

Question 2: Is Death My Way Out?

> Will you work wonders for the dead?
>   Shall the dead arise and praise you? Selah
> Shall your lovingkindness be declared in the grave,
>   or your faithfulness in the place of destruction?
> Shall your wonders be known in the dark?
>   And your righteousness in the land of forgetfulness?
> LORD, why do you cast off my soul?
>   Why do you hide your face from me?
> (Ps. 88:10–12, 14)

I've already introduced you to this psalm and by now you know it is a song. If you were to do a complete read through of this psalm (and I hope you've already done so), "song" may not be the first thing that comes to your mind. Much like Asaph in Psalm 77, this psalm is penned as a melodic, corporate lament. And there are six questions posed by the psalmist, six questions focused on deliverance in death. This is holy sorrow. These questions, offered to the Lord, are just as carefully and thoughtfully crafted as the psalms of praise. In fact, this particular psalm showcases a well-roundedness in the life of God's people. Solomon did in fact say there is a time for everything (Eccl. 3:4).

Psalm 88 was drafted and sung for the purpose of weeping and mourning melodically (don't think country song, though). The questions posed by the psalmists can be seen as a plead to God for a speedy recovery. The musing of the psalmist is this: a living man delivered from his ailments is better than a dead man delivered from his ailments. This psalm is a song for our suffering. And not just a song, but it teaches us that requests can be made to the Lord regarding our sufferings. For Christians this means we worship the Lord who has the power to deliver us in our weeping and mourning just as we worship him with our laughing and dancing. These are the seasons of our lives. God has equipped us well for the ups and downs of living in a fallen world. For those of us wrestling with depression, we really can ask the Lord questions about our deliverance with worshipful hearts. Now, in these few verses, I want you to notice that these questions had three underlying concerns: present faithful worship of the Lord, a testimony of the Lord's faithfulness, and deliverance from the present condition/situation.

First, these psalmists were committed to worshipping the Lord even in a desperate, isolated season. Even if they weren't delivered, they would worship. The fact this psalm exists is a testimony to that. In fact, their weakness and suffering drove them into deeper communion with God. Suffering, when viewed appropriately, enriches worship. We should not desire to suffer, but we can enjoy intimacy with God in our suffering. A while ago, the power went out at our house at night. One of my sons was going through a season of being scared of the dark. He was scared of what he couldn't see or articulate. He hears what he perceives to be threatening noises at night. So, to help him, we installed some nightlights and a noise machine. The problem is, when the power went out, so did the nightlights and noise machine. So around 1:00 am, my son ran as fast as he could into our bedroom in an effort to outrun the darkness. He fled to safety. He came to his mother and me. Now, did I coldly send him back to his room? I picked him up in the darkness and held him tight. In fact, I squeezed him a bit to let him know he was secure and safe even though he couldn't

Ask Questions in Faith

see. After realizing the power was out, I let him sleep with us and he slept hard. He felt safe. I didn't eliminate the darkness. I didn't drown out the threatening noises that take advantage of his imagination. I held him close. He looked to me for security and safety. He drew near to me, and I received him. I kept him until the sun came up. I was with him in the darkness. My son came to me in his distress, and I was with him in the thick of it.

The psalmists drew near to God in what may have been the darkest season of their lives and these questions are evidences of that. Psalm 88 is certainly one of the saddest chapters in Scripture as we saw in chapter 3. And if nothing else, this psalm, this song, declares the dependence of the psalmist and the corporate body of believers on the Lord. The night was at its darkest and they turned to the Lord who is sovereign over the darkness. They turned to the one who has overcome the darkness (John 1:5).

This psalm could have gone in another direction. The psalmists could have drifted into despair fueled by an uncertainty regarding the character and Word of God. These questions could have become statements declaring God couldn't deliver them even in death. The questions could have been driven by a sort of self-pity, in which man and his circumstances are bigger than the God who created the cosmos, stepped into this world, and conquered death, hell, and the grave.[55] In Bunyan's *Pilgrim's Progress*, we see despair grip Christian and Hopeful after they determined there was a better, easier, and more expedient way than the way of the King of the Celestial City:

> The Giant [Despair] pushed them [Christian and Hopeful] in front of him and put them into his Castle [of doubt], into

---

[55] While not directly related to the topic at hand, the root issue with despair I believe is an improper view of God. A book I often recommend to people I counsel is Ed Welch's book, *When People Are Big and God Is Small: Overcoming Peer Pressure, Codependency, and the Fear of Man* (Philipsburg, NJ: P&R Publishing, 1997). In this book, Welch takes the reader by the hand and reorients their perspective toward the Lord.

a very dark Dungeon, nasty and stinking to the spirits of these two men. They laid there from Wednesday morning until Saturday night, without one bit of bread, or drop of drink, or light, or anyone asking how they did. They were far from friends and acquaintance. It was in this place that Christian had double the sorrow, because it was through his unadvised haste that they were brought into this distress.[56]

Depression can lead to despair if we begin to doubt that God and his ways are good. Depression can lead to despair when we try to manipulate or control circumstances beyond our control. Humility is key. Christian and Hopeful sought comfort over obedience. Ease over worship. They believed they could short-cut God's journey for them because they began to believe they knew better than God and this led to "double the sorrow." The psalmists could have had double the sorrow had they not cried out to the Lord who was present in the midst of the darkness. The psalmist could have had double the sorrow had they not worshipfully asked questions to God. Despair comes knocking on the door for those of us who have experienced the lowest pit. But speaking to God through questions of faith from the depths of the pit preserves us from godless despair.

Secondly, the psalmists were concerned about the testimony of the Lord. They were committed to giving God the glory for deliverance, when God delivered it according to his timetable. This is one of the reasons they wanted to be delivered in life and not in death. Don't forget that the psalmists are communing with God in the midst of their dire circumstances while leading a congregation in communion with God. They are publicly worshipping the Lord in grief and leading a congregation in how to worship in grief. If these psalmists and the assembly were concerned about the testimony of the Lord during this dark season of life, how

---

[56] Bunyan, *The Pilgrim's Progress*, 160–161.

Ask Questions in Faith

much more will the Sons of Korah and the congregation give glory to God for his deliverance of them in life? In distress and in deliverance, they will testify to God's faithfulness. They will testify of his wonders and righteousness. This is tremendous. How many examples do we have in church history and perhaps even in our present lives of people who expanded the kingdom of God on earth as it is in heaven because of their singular focus to glorify him through their suffering? The very Word of God was written by men who suffered immensely. Their very blood and suffering advances the news of Christ's Lordship over all things.

Think of Shadrach, Meshach, and Abed-Nego and their experience in Babylon. In maybe one of the most familiar stories in the Scripture, these three men refused to forsake their worship of the one true and living God even if it cost them their comfort and their very lives.

> Now if you are ready at the time you hear the sound of the horn, flute, harp, lyre, *and* psaltery, in symphony with all kinds of music, and you fall down and worship the image which I have made, *good!* But if you do not worship, you shall be cast immediately into the midst of a burning fiery furnace. And who *is* the god who will deliver you from my hands? Shadrach, Meshach, and Abed-Nego answered and said to the king, "O Nebuchadnezzar, we have no need to answer you in this matter. If that *is the case*, our God whom we serve is able to deliver us from the burning fiery furnace, and he will deliver *us* from your hand, O king. But if not, let it be known to you, O king, that we do not serve your gods, nor will we worship the gold image which you have set up."

In deliverance, torture, or death, these men were committed to the Lord. Their devotion to him and commitment to testify *about* him even in Babylon were not contingent on their well-being. In life and death these men were kept by an unchanging God who sustained their very souls. The same was true for the psalmists. The

The Day of Trouble

same is true for you. Be concerned about the testimony of the Lord in your life as you faithfully worship and submit to him in your struggle.

However, this confidence and contentment in the Lord and our commitment to promoting his Lordship should not prevent us from asking to be delivered. An emotional plea to be delivered is the third thing we need to see underneath these questions. A friend recently told me that when he prays, he says, "I know you will do this (deliver me) *or something much better.*"[57] The psalmists *asked* to be delivered. In chapter 3, I demonstrated how Psalm 88 could be read with Christ in mind. Christ *prayed* for deliverance, but he knew the "better" his suffering would accomplish, and he stayed the course. Shadrach, Meshach, and Abed-Nego did *not* want to be thrown into a furnace and burned alive, but they stayed the course. In the same way, we should not call suffering good, nor should we seek suffering as some monastic form of penance or fail to pray for deliverance from suffering. Underneath the questions of the psalmists is a sincere desire to be delivered from pain. Suffering is evil. Suffering entered humanity after the fall of Adam. God did not declare suffering as good. Therefore, it is right and acceptable to want to be delivered from it. Believer, it is okay to want to be delivered from depression so long as deliverance remains in its proper place—*at the feet of our sovereign and wise King.* Because while suffering is not good, God does use suffering for our good (Gen. 50:20). We do not suffer meaninglessly. Can you think of anything more miserable than meaningless suffering? Our suffering is evil, but our good, wise, powerful Triune God who makes demons tremble (Ja. 2:19) turns evil on its head as a pawn in his cosmic plan and uses it for his glory and our eternal benefit. God is building us for a sweet eternity with him and he uses our suffering as one of the tools to build us. This means,

---

[57] My friend attributes this to author and theologian John Piper, although I have not been able to locate the source.

Ask Questions in Faith

that while we can and should pray to be delivered as the authors of Psalm 88 did, we can have confidence and hope that our Sovereign God is using our suffering in a good, holy way.

Conclusion

The Lord is present as we suffer, and he is using all things (even our depression) to fashion us as a potter does with clay (Jer. 18; Rom. 9:21). And with that grounding reality we can ask questions in faith to remind ourselves of his goodness, kindness, his mercy and grace. And all of these attributes of his are unchanging because he is his attributes.

Dear reader, our good God, the "I Am" (Ex. 3:14) determined to send Jesus, the suffering Savior on behalf of his elect. The Holy Spirit then gave Christ's righteousness to God's people *freely*. You see, God determined to be merciful and near to you before the foundation of the world. Let me put this another way: before you were created, God set you apart for salvation, sanctification, and glorification. If you're a Christian, you have been adopted into God's family. This wasn't because God peaked into the future and saw that you'd make good choices. He chose you before the foundation of the world because he wanted to. This means that your salvation, your suffering, your comfort, your perseverance is in the hands of your sovereign, good God. So, take heart. *You* aren't a fortress. *You* aren't ok on your own. You needed outside intervention, and God acted in Christ. The Lord alone is your fortress. He surrounds you. He protects you. He guards you. In the fog of depression, it is easy to forget that. In the next chapter we are going to look at how corporate worship—the public gathering of God's saints can be used by God to minister to us in the thick of our depression. And while I don't want to get ahead of myself, there is one aspect of public worship that I would like to further connect to the psalms we've been examining (hopefully you al-

The Day of Trouble

ready see the connection clearly) and that is singing. Never underestimate the power and presence of God when you sing with God's church. The Lord uses music to shape us and help us recall the glorious, fixed truths we already know, but have often forgot. When we are having a difficult time remembering, we should sing. That may sound counterintuitive, but it is good for us and dare I use the word therapeutic? And while singing alone is good, singing with the gathered saints is glorious—a glimpse of heaven.

Perhaps this is why Asaph was the chief temple musician. Perhaps this is why the Sons of Korah wrote the song of Psalm 88. Maybe this is why the Psalms of Lament are actually the *Songs* of Lament. Songs have the ability to remind us forgetful, weary travelers of important unchanging truths about our Triune God and consequently about us. There is one particular hymn that has meant more to me in my fight against depression and various sufferings than any other hymn I know. The hymn is called "A Mighty Fortress is Our God." It was written in the 1500s by the Reformer, Martin Luther. The song is a paraphrase of Psalm 46. I often meditate on the lyrics and our church sings this song regularly. And I can't help but to think that Luther wrote this song to console himself in the midst of a depressed season of life. Take in these words, dear struggler, as we close out this chapter:

> A mighty fortress is our God,
> a bulwark never failing;
> Our helper he, amid the flood
> of mortal ills prevailing:
> for still our ancient foe
> doth seek to work us woe;
> his craft and pow'r are great,
> and, armed with cruel hate,
> on earth is not his equal.

Ask Questions in Faith

And though this world, with devils filled,
should threaten to undo us,
we will not fear, for God hath willed
his truth to triumph through us;
the Prince of Darkness grim,
we tremble not for him;
his rage we can endure, for lo, his doom is sure,
one little word shall fell him.

That word above all earthly pow'rs,
no thanks to them, abideth;
the Spirit and the gifts are ours
through him who with us sideth;
let goods and kindred go,
this mortal life also;
the body they may kill:
God's truth abideth still,
his kingdom is forever.

Discuss and Apply
1. Adopt the questions of Psalms 77 and 88 and wrestle with your answers. Do they match the answers of the psalmists who asked them in faith?
2. What questions of faith can *you* ask in the midst of your depression?
3. How does the immutability of God give you hope in your struggle with depression?
4. Meditate on Numbers 23:19; Isaiah 40:8; Hebrews 13:8; and James 1:17 and write one practical takeaway from each passage.

Chapter 5
Combatting Depression Through Corporate Worship[58]

Thomas Watson once said that "God has twisted together his glory and our good."[59] I've read that quote from Watson a lot. I've done so because it is immensely comforting to me especially on dark days. That the God of the cosmos would intertwine his glory and my good—namely my salvation, is humbling and encouraging to me. And my aim in this chapter is to demonstrate that beautiful and true statement by encouraging you to glorify God in corporate worship even in the midst of your depression because your good and his glory are "twisted together." Corporate Worship can be a powerful weapon in the day of trouble—in the cave of depression. I would argue that God *primarily* strengthens you through the preaching of his Word, corporate prayer, and the sacraments[60] that remind us of our union with Christ, our connection to his bride—the church, and just how transformative and far reaching the gospel of God is. It is so good for us, especially in our depressive down swings, to gather with God's blood bought church. Yet,

---

[58] I do want to make clear that the focus of corporate worship is the glory of God, his gospel, and the building of his church. So, while I am connecting the benefit of corporate worship for one suffering with depression, I do not want this most important truth to be lost on us. Furthermore, one of the reasons I am emphasizing corporate worship in this book is because God especially promises to be with us and grow us when we gather with his people (Ps. 87:2; Matt. 18:20, Col. 2:2; 3:16).

[59] Thomas Watson, *Body of Divinity*, 21.

[60] This is what theologians call *Media gratia* (Means of Grace) and it refers to those specific means God has appointed for your growth in the grace of Christ Jesus. As we avail ourselves of these means, the Holy Spirit of God nurtures us in the gospel. For a fantastic primer on this subject, check out: J. Ryan Davidson, *Green Pastures: A Primer on the Ordinary Means of Grace* (Palmdale, CA: RBAP, 2019).

a recent Barna study demonstrates many people's disbelief (or discontent) that God uses these means to conform us more into the image of Christ.[61] Barna reports a decline in church membership among young people, and in their survey defined "practicing Christians" as those who gather for worship at least once a month and "churched adults" as those who participate every six months. A study like this really does demonstrate a low view of what a "practicing" Christian is and a low priority on God's weekly gathering. Could it be that we lack trust and patience in the efficacy of God's ways (in which he gives of himself according to his means) to actually comfort, convict, and conform us according to his will?

So far in our journey together, we've discussed symptoms, causes, and adopting the language of the psalmists to describe and address our depression. In the last chapter we worked through the necessity of asking questions in faith so that we can remember the sovereignty, immutability, and goodness of God. In *this* chapter we will further develop a strategy to mount a war against our depressive disposition. This strategy, plainly said is a challenge to commit to worshipping God with his gathering—the local church.

Lord's Day Worship[62]
Dear brother or sister struggling on this long road of depression—guard Sundays for you and your family because it is a foundational habit you need to establish and is especially beneficial as the waves of depression crash over you. Just as Peter needed to look at Christ as he walked to him in stormy waters (Matt. 14:22–33), so too do we need to see Christ with the eyes of faith in the stormy

---

[61] Barna's *State of the Church 2020* demonstrates this point.

[62] This chapter does assume that you are a member in good standing at a healthy, God-centered, orthodox local church. If you are not a part of a local church, begin your search by exploring websites and doctrinal statements and the sermons of a church near you. Then, go visit a church. I recommend visiting a church for at least a month before you make a decision about checking out another church or committing in membership with the one you are visiting.

Corporate Worship

sea of depression. Gathering with God's church on Sundays is the primary way God puts Christ in focus for you. Gathering for worship is a good ancient practice commanded of us by God. Since the bodily resurrection of Christ, God's church has come together each Sunday to be reminded through the proclamation of the Word, corporate prayer, and sacrament that she worships a living, Triune God who ordained her salvation before the foundation of the world, accomplished her salvation in Jesus, and sealed her salvation by the power of the Holy Spirit. On our best days, we are forgetful of the sustaining work of the Triune God, so how much more do we need to be reminded through these means when our forgetfulness is compounded by our depression?

We need to hear from Charles Spurgeon again. Spurgeon was no stranger to depression. He suffered with this affliction immensely and his very words on the gathering of God's church should be a testimony to us of someone who wrestled with depression until he died yet prioritized the gathered assembly of the saints. Spurgeon says,

> We gather together on the first rather than the seventh day of the week because redemption is even a greater work than creation and more worthy of commemoration and because the rest which followed creation is far outdone by the rest which ensues upon the completion of redemption. Like the Apostles, we meet on the first day of the week and hope that Jesus may stand in our midst and say, "Peace be unto you." Our Lord has lifted the Sabbath from the old and rusty hinges where on the law had placed it long before and set it on the new golden hinges which His love has fashioned. He has placed our rest day not at the end of a week of toil but at the beginning of the rest which remains for the people of God. Every first day of the week we should meditate on the

rising of our Lord and seek to enter into the fellowship with him in His risen life.[63]

Did you hear what Spurgeon said? Every Sunday is Easter Sunday. Every Sunday we gather because Christ resurrected in *this* world and acquired for us peace (Col. 1:20) and rest (Matt. 11:28–30). Those that struggle with depression are looking for peace and rest. The resurrected Jesus gives peace and rest to his gathered church because he is peace and rest and he is spiritually present with the church as they gather around him through the Word, prayer, and sacrament (Rev. 1:12–13). Cultivating a habit of corporate worship where the means of grace are faithfully practiced is your starting place for combatting depression. Every other godly habit you develop follows from *this* habit. Therefore, let's look at how we can best avail ourselves of the Word, prayer, and sacrament in our effort to combat depression and find peace and rest in Jesus.

The Word
Bible intake on the Lord's Day comes in several ways: reading the Word, preaching the Word, singing the Word, praying the Word, and speaking the Word to one another in fellowship. The most significant way to hear God's Word is through weekly preaching. While technology allows us to listen to sermons online, we primarily hear the Word preached each Lord's Day in *community with other believers*.[64] During the time of the Reformers, Christians believed that to hear the Word rightly interpreted and preached by a faithful pastor on Sunday was to hear God himself. You become like the preaching you sit under, and the Lord can

---

[63] C.H. Spurgeon, *Spurgeon's Sermons on the Death and Resurrection of Jesus* (Peabody, MA: Hendrickson, 2005), 572.

[64] Martyn Lloyd-Jones believed so much in the supernatural work of the Spirit in preaching among God's gathered assembly that he did not want his sermons to be recorded because he knew that technology could never substitute being present with the assembly. Members of his church recorded him anyways.

Corporate Worship

use a faithful exposition of Scripture to help renew your mind and certainly your emotions. The Holy Spirit of God really does use his preached Word in your inner man despite your wobbly knees, and cloudy downcast mind. But this does beg the question, "How can we commit ourselves to being attentive during preaching?" Those of us that wrestle with depression are prone toward being distracted and fatigued and may need to be more intentional as we sit under the preaching of the Word.

A good first step of intentionality is a commitment to prayer as we hear God's Word. We want humble, receptive hearts remembering that God's Word accomplishes in us what God purposed it to (Isa. 55:11). As the Bible is opened and proclaimed, receive it by asking for the Holy Spirit to help you understand and obey it. Another practical step is to bring a hard copy of the Bible, a notepad, and pen. I don't like using my Bible app on my phone because I may receive text messages or calls during the corporate worship service and this will be a distraction (not only to you, but others around you). At my local church we provide a worship guide with notes for people inclined toward taking notes and we've found this useful for most people. When I listen to a sermon, I use a blank piece of paper and write down everything that stands out to me as I hear the preacher exposit the Word. Later, I'm able to take that note sheet and prayerfully ask the following questions:

- How does this sermon help me savor Christ more?
- What heart idols did this exposition reveal?
- What does this passage of Scripture require of me?
- What Scripture or point in the sermon should I meditate on this week?
- How should the sermon shape my prayer life for the week?
- How should the sermon shape my public witness for Jesus?

The Day of Trouble

Asking questions like this can help ensure we are hearing, retaining, and obeying God's Word well. This coming Sunday take your Bible, a pen, and paper and prayerfully listen to the sufficient Scripture being preached knowing the Lord is using it to strengthen you.[65]

Corporate singing is another means God uses to proclaim Scripture or at least the rich doctrines of Scripture. The songs of the gathered church admonish us to hope in Christ Jesus (Eph. 5:19; Col. 3:16). Everyone needs to be admonished in the Word, but to be admonished by singing saints is a balm to a struggling soul. The psalms we have looked at in this book have been for many years sang in the assembly. There is something about making much of God through song even if we are filled with sorrow. For me, singing feels like what I am supposed to do when some glorious truth burns in me. It's also what I yearn to do in my grief—when I am depressed. Music has the power to transport us to this world that feels so familiar, but that we've never been to. Perhaps it's the land Frodo dreamt of in Bombadil's house—a far green country with lots of singing.[66] Or even better, the one John spoke of while on the island of Patmos (Rev. 21:1–5). Early on in John's vision, we see him hang his head in a depressive state and sob— some translations say "wept bitterly" or "wept much" (Rev. 5:4). The situation was dire because there was no one found in heaven, on earth, or under the earth who could open the scroll (the deed of man's inheritance—the Lamb's Book of Life). And just as John was on the verge of utter despair, one of the elders told him to look at the Lion of Judah (v. 5). As John looked, he saw that this Lion, King Jesus, is the only one with the authority

---

[65] Christopher Ash has an excellent booklet on how to listen to a sermon. The book is called *Listen Up! A Practical Guide to Listening to Sermons* (Charlotte NC: The Good Book Company, 2009). One step he gives that is so lost on us in this digital age is to listen to a sermon *in church*.

[66] J.R.R. Tolkien, *The Fellowship of the Ring* (Boston, MA: Houghton Mifflin, 1986), 146.

Corporate Worship

to open the scroll and give man the inheritance earned by Christ. And upon John gazing at Christ—this faithful Lion-Lamb, and seeing all of this, what happens? Everyone begins to sing a new song about the worthiness of Christ and the far-reaching nature of his blood (vv. 8–10). John went from this deep, dark, depressive state to gazing on Christ, to singing.

In corporate singing we preach one collective sermon to each other and through melody, say, "set your gaze on Christ. He is alone is worthy. He alone is your peace. He alone is your rest." And this is eternally true my dear downcast believer. And while you don't have the visions of the Apostle John, you have the Holy Spirit who inspired those words inside of you (1 Cor. 6:19). You have his words kept pure for you. You have the songs of the saints throughout all ages. You have 2000 years of church history. And you have your local church to help you remember who you are in Christ and most importantly remember who he is. The Apostle Paul says, "Let the word of Christ dwell in you richly in all wisdom, teaching and admonishing one another in psalms and hymns and spiritual songs, singing with grace in your hearts to the Lord" (Col. 3:16). In corporate singing we stand up as our brothers and sisters have down all through history with God's gathered saints out of the cave of depression, look other believers in the eyes and comfort each other by singing to our worthy Savior. In the midst of our depressions, anxieties, sins, and sufferings we can be comforted by extolling God with our spiritual family, the bride of Christ. So dear brothers and sisters, *sing*. Though your voice quivers, and the tears keep coming, *sing*. Sing *of* your King. Sing *to* your King. Sing to be reminded. He *is* coming back. He is coming back to make an end to everything bad.

Prayer
Prayer is another means of grace given to us by God. And one of

the encouraging things about prayer is how practical it is. God really does use the prayers of his people to accomplish his eternal decree. In prayer, we can humble ourselves before our Creator and cast our very anxieties on him because our Creator cares for us (1 Pt. 5:6–7). Think for a moment of the goodness of God in that he desires to hear our prayers. Our sovereign God who created the heavens and the earth and sustains it by the Word of his power (Heb. 1:3) is also near to us and even in the midst of our depression *hears* us. Now, you learn how to pray primarily by doing it. When most of us think of prayer, we think of private prayer (which I will address in the next chapter). While private prayer is good and should be practiced, I believe our private prayers flow first from our commitment to (you guessed it) *corporate* prayer. Not only that, but they are shaped by it. In corporate prayer we learn the privilege of speaking *to* God, how to commune with him, the importance of confessing our adoration, thankfulness, sins, sufferings, petitions, and how to do that consistently.

At our local church, we pray in our service. We pray to speak *to* God and not as a means to transition to another part of the service and we pray that teaches our church to focus in prayer. We don't want it to be an afterthought or a mindless ritual. Those who wrestle with depression need to develop a focused prayer life. It is taking Christ up on his invitation to enter into his rest (Matt. 11:28–30). We also open our worship service with a prayer after reading from a selection of Scripture. This teaches us that we hear from God by reading his Word and his Word shapes our prayers—much like we saw with the psalms. But that is our rhythm: hear God's Word and respond by speaking to him. Every week we also have a time of confession of sin. It is here that we confess particular sins to God based on a passage for that week. For the believer who may be depressed because of unconfessed sin, developing a habit of confessing sin (and repenting of it) is a return to joy (Ps. 51:12). Our confession of sin is always in light of the pardon

Corporate Worship

we have received in Christ. You can and should participate in corporate prayer. It is there where you not only learn how to pray, but you actually pray with an assembly of believers who are sufferers and sinners on this short, but hard pilgrimage. Be with God's people and pray.

Lord's Supper
God preaches the gospel to us using pictures.[67] He gave us two pictures called *sacraments* to observe in the context of the local church whereby we announce the finished work of Christ and that we belong to him. These sacraments are the Lord's Supper and baptism. The Gospel of Matthew speaks of Christ's institution of the Lord's Supper and in it we see several gospel implications that demonstrate the necessity and goodness of this important meal:

> And as they were eating, Jesus took bread, blessed and broke *it*, and gave *it* to the disciples and said, "Take, eat; this is My body." Then He took the cup, and gave thanks, and gave *it* to them, saying, "Drink from it, all of you. For this is My blood of the new covenant, which is shed for many for the remission of sins. But I say to you, I will not drink of this fruit of the vine from now on until that day when I drink it new with you in My Father's kingdom." (Matt. 26:26–29)

As we feast on the Lord's Supper, we are confessing our *union* with Christ made possible by *his* sufferings. We are in him. He is in us. Our struggles with depression cannot divide this sacred union. As the bread and wine touch our tongue, we are declaring the supernatural work of the Holy Spirit uniting us fallen, sinful, broken people with the perfect person and work of Jesus. No matter our circumstances our lives really are hidden with Christ in God (Col. 3:3). It is good to be reminded of Christ's sufferings through

---

[67] They are much more than pictures of course.

this sacrament. The danger in suffering is that we may only see ourselves as sufferers. We all have blinders, and we all tend to put our sufferings in high definition and in doing so fall into despair and become embittered. Our Instagram saturated society has further cemented this. What we tend to see of other people online is mostly fictitious. Yet even though we may know that, our overindulgence in things like social media further drive home the lie that we alone suffer and we brood as we covet the lives of all the happy people in the world. The Lord's Supper provides us an opportunity to think of the sufferings of another Person. Jesus was the "man of sorrows and acquainted with grief" (Isa. 53:3) beyond anything we could ever experience or imagine. The anguish, isolation, betrayal, crucifixion, and descent should humble us and give us perspective at his table. And as that bread and wine humble us we rightly turn and worship him. I am so thankful the Lord's Supper gets our eyes off our ourselves and on the redemptive sufferings of Christ.

As we eat this meal, we are also declaring the *sufficient* work of Jesus. There is nothing left for Christ to do to accomplish our salvation. Some struggling with depression wrestle with their assurance of faith. They feel missed, abandoned, or disqualified from the gospel of God. The Lord's Supper preaches a different message to us. On the cross Jesus cried out "It is finished" (John 19:28–30). Jesus didn't accomplish 90% of the work and leave us with a remaining 10% to complete. Christ accomplished everything God's holy justice required for our salvation. The need has been met. God's righteous wrath was satisfied. Our salvation was accomplished and is sustained based on Christ alone and not ourselves. Those in Christ are secure in him. In fact, the Holy Spirit of God is the guarantor of our inheritance (Eph. 1:14). As we observe this meal, we are remembering not only the physical agony Christ endured, but also the preserving work of his sacrifice for us. The author of Hebrews says that when Jesus himself purged our sins, he sat down at the right hand of God (Heb. 1:3). Our salvation is eternally accomplished in Christ. Jesus bore the wrath of God for our sin and he did so sufficiently. We remember this every time we take this meal and it should encourage us.

Finally, as we participate in the Lord's Supper, we are reminded that we will *dine* with Christ in the new heavens and new earth (more on the new heavens and new earth in the conclusion). Jesus told his disciples, "I will not drink of this fruit of the vine from now on until that day when I drink it new with you in My Father's kingdom" (Matt. 26:29). I am not sure of all that this passage means, but the Lord's Supper has clear eschatological implications. As we regularly eat this meal, we are reminded that Jesus will share this meal with us when he returns. One day you and I will take this meal with Christ without any sin, any depression, any conflict, and any shame. We will take it with Jesus without *any* hindrances. We will take it with those saints and loved ones who have died in Christ. We will take it with Christ not just spiritually present, but physically present. Think of the hope that stirs inside of a believer who thinks their depression will never end. As the meal is set before us, we can have confidence that there is a day that is sure to come because the one who resurrected from the grave said we would dine with him in his kingdom. *One day.*

Jesus instituted this soul nourishing meal to remind us of all these things in picture form. Why would we neglect it? This ordinary means of grace is good for us. This meal is for you, depressed Christian. Eat and drink.

Baptism
Like the Lord's Supper, the sacrament of baptism preaches to us in picture form reminding us of several important, unchanging gospel realities. Again, the Gospel of Matthew records the instructions of Jesus regarding baptism in 28:18–20:

The Day of Trouble

And Jesus came and spoke to them, saying, "All authority has been given to Me in heaven and on earth. Go therefore and make disciples of all the nations, baptizing them in the name of the Father and of the Son and of the Holy Spirit, teaching them to observe all things that I have commanded you; and lo, I am with you always, *even* to the end of the age." Amen.

First, we are reminded that disciples are made through the *authority* of Jesus. Abraham Kuyper, said at his inaugural address at the Free University of Amsterdam, "There is not a square inch in the whole domain of our human existence over which Christ, who is Sovereign over all, does not cry, Mine!"[68] In baptism we are reminded of the authority of Christ. The person being baptized is only getting baptized because Christ has all authority. Christ has authority in what is not seen (heaven) and over what is seen (earth or your depression). The pastor giving a Trinitarian baptism can only do so because Christ has authority over all. As we sit and watch new believers in Jesus go into the water a sermon is being preached to us that all things are under the sovereign authority of Christ. For a believer struggling with depression, they can fall into thinking and operating as if they are enslaved to the negative emotions they feel. Every single antidepressant commercial I've ever seen gives the depressed person the body posture of one who is enslaved and utterly defeated. Now, this may be exactly how you feel, but this feeling has no grounding in reality. The same Christ who has authority over every square inch of creation has authority over your depression too. He is more powerful than the strongest wave of emotion. The next time you see a brother or sister baptized, remember that Christ has all authority.

---

[68] Abraham Kuyper, *Abraham Kuyper: a Centennial Reader*, ed. James D. Bratt (Grand Rapids, MI: Eerdmans, 1998), 488.

Corporate Worship

Second, we remember and confess through baptism that our God is *Trinity*. We baptize in the name of the Father, Son, and Holy Spirit. Because God is Trinity he does not rule from a distance. In our depressed emotions, we may feel he is distant, but all of redemptive history tells us otherwise. In God's kindness he condescended to us in the person and work of Jesus who is our High Priest who can sympathize with our weaknesses (Heb. 4:15). In God's kindness he deposited his Comforter, the Holy Spirit (*paraclete*) in us and provides for us that "peace that surpasses all understanding" (Phil. 4:7) and guards our hearts and minds. We also experience the nearness of God by being with the body of Christ as we collectively witness the baptism of a new believer. Believer, you are not alone. Our God is near and he makes his nearness known to you.

Third, through baptism we are reminded to *obey*. When your lost in the fog of depression, you can be more susceptible toward sin. Through baptism we are reminded that disciples obey what God has commanded. Baptism itself is really one of the first acts of obedience in the life of a new believer marking a desire to be one who obeys in response to the finished work of Christ. Our depression does not give us license to sin—whether that is a sin of omission or commission. Christians, despite their emotions, are to obey all that King Jesus has commanded us to obey. And because we are new creatures in Christ and have the indwelling Holy Spirit, we can exhibit self-control (Gal. 5:22–23), take our thoughts captive (1 Cor. 10:5) and seek to honor the Lord despite our depressed emotions.

Conclusion
Hopefully at this stage in our journey together you are convinced of the priority and usefulness of corporate worship to combat your depression. It is in that particular gathering every Sunday that God promises to change you through the ordinary means of

grace—Word, prayer, and sacrament. The question is, do you trust his methods? Are you willing to submit to his prescribed means to be built up in Christ even as you wrestle this side of eternity with your downcast emotions? Do you see that the spiritual presence of Christ with his gathered church really can minister to you in the midst of your depression? My struggling friend, submit yourself to the Word preached, sung, prayed, and pictured in sacrament. And be reminded that the Lord God is near.

Discuss and Apply
1. How committed are you to your local church? Are you a member? How often do you attend? Are you known?
2. What practical steps do you take each week to ensure you engage with corporate worship?
3. Do you consider yourself a "doer" of the Word? (Ja. 1:2–25)
4. What means did God promise to use to conform us more into the image of Jesus? Are you taking advantage of those means?
5. How has this chapter shaped the way you think of the sacraments?

Chapter 6
Combatting Depression Through Spiritual Disciplines

What are your habits? Think about it for a moment. All of us develop, intentionally and unintentionally, deep-seated rhythms in our lives. For some of us these rhythms are helpful and for others they're destructive. In church culture we say the word *discipline* a lot. Discipline comes from the Latin word, *discipulus* from which we get the word *disciple*. A disciple is a committed follower—a diligent student dedicated to a teacher and to what is taught. This is helpful for us because the very definition of this word tells us that our habits (disciplines) necessitate a disciple-*maker*. For Christians, we are disciples of Jesus. Therefore, our habits should reflect our following of him. Our disciplines should magnify Christ (Ja. 2:14–26). However, for many of us our habits indicate we have a different disciple-maker; a different master; a different savior. Therefore, I want to frame this chapter by asking you a question: Who do your habits say your master is? Who is the savior you embrace when the tsunami of depression crashes down on you? I spent the last chapter demonstrating to you the importance of the ordinary means of grace in corporate worship as a primary way to combat your depression.[69] In this chapter I want to spend time on how you can wage daily war on your depression through intentional God-centered spiritual disciplines because battling

---

[69] I do not want to assume that this goes without saying, but while corporate worship in my view is the primary way to combat depression, the focus of corporate worship is not the healing of your depression. The focus of corporate worship is the glory of the Triune God and the building of his church. We must maintain that fundamental perspective on God's assembly.

depression is about submitting to *the* master and submitting to Christ as master requires regular, spiritual disciplines.

Fear God Not Your Depression
Every Christian should cultivate the fear of God in their lives and we do this through daily spiritual disciplines. In fact, it is through regular spiritual disciplines that we even truly learn what it means to fear God. Fearing God is vital. We either fear God or we are devoured by our enemies. Sadly, though the fear of God is such a foreign concept that it goes neglected in our lives and we suffer as a result. For example, when I ask people how I can pray for them, they often respond with a request for things like wisdom, knowledge, or understanding. And the request usually relates to a very specific situation. In Proverbs, King Solomon talks about these sorts of attributes, but they are tethered to what people do not ask for in a prayer request: the fear of God (2:5). And I would argue that cultivating a fear of God is exactly what the doctor ordered for those of us on the war-torn chaotic path of depression. Fearing God is much better than fearing depression. Fearing God is good. Fearing depression is evil. When you fear the Lord, it sets your struggle with depression in its proper place. Instead of seeing your depression as the big, unconquerable enemy, you begin to see it under the rule and reign of the Triune God. Even the darkness is like bright light to our good, sovereign, powerful God (Ps. 139:12). But, before I go further, allow me to define what it means to fear God because that may be an unfamiliar phrase to some of you. That word *fear* (יִרְאָה) in Hebrew has in view the holiness of God. He is not a God to be trifled with. He *is* gravitas and those in rebellion to God and his word should fear him because they will be judged by him based on their biographies (Rev. 20:11–15). But for those who belong to the Lord to fear him means to reverence him in gratitude, devotion, and worship. For the believer, the fear of the Lord is an experiential, warm, devoted, and reverent heart

Spiritual Disciplines

posture that desires to worship and obey God no matter the sacrifice. The kind of Christian that fears the Lord is one who's thinking, emotions, and worship is regulated by Scripture.[70] Therefore, for our purposes in this book we should see that cultivating the fear of the Lord is essential to not fear and thus be paralyzed by depression. And fearing the Lord comes from our God-centered habits —our spiritual disciplines.

A Word-Centered Life Leads to a God-Centered Life
A good place to begin personally developing God-centered habits is reading God's Word. The Scripture is central to the godly habits we seek to establish. And in order to read God's Word effectively, we must have the right tools and a plan. First, you need a translation you can understand. I personally read from the *New King James Version*, but many of the people at the church I pastor read from the *English Standard Version* (ESV). I recommend you begin with a readable translation especially if you're new to reading Scripture. And as a side note, don't get the cheapest Bible you can find. If you plan to spend years reading your Bible, invest money in a Bible in which the binding and cover will last. Also, eye fatigue is a real issue with some of the cheaply made Bibles due to font size, color of the paper, and spacing. Purchase a nice Bible that is designed well for reading and do not be afraid to write in it. If you need help finding the right type of Bible, ask your pastor to help you.[71]

I would also encourage you to get a Bible commentary. You need a faithful, wise, tutor readily accessible as you read your Bible. You have that on Sundays as your pastor explains the Word to you, but you need one throughout the week as you make a habit

---

[70] The Baptist puritan, John Bunyan says in his excellent book *The Fear of God* (Edinburgh: Banner of Truth Trust, 2018) that the Word of God is the rule and director of our fear.

[71] The *Reformation Study Bible* put out by Ligonier is excellent. The commentary notes are helpful, the cross references in it are thoughtful.

The Day of Trouble

of reading God's Word. Growing up, my dad introduced me to Matthew Henry's commentary. There is a one volume version of this commentary you can purchase for under 25 bucks. I still use it to this day. Henry's commentary is expositional and devotional and it's a perfect companion for your Bible reading. It is said that the great evangelist of the 18th-century, George Whitfield, read his Bible with Matthew Henry's commentary regularly. There are many people in the local church I pastor that find Henry's commentaries to be excellent helps in their devotional reading and studying.

Once you have the tools, you need a *plan*. In conversations with people about Bible reading I am often surprised at how few people have a reading plan. Statistically speaking, if you do not have a Bible reading plan, you will not consistently read the Bible. Presently I read through the Bible chronologically each year. I have been doing this for a few years now and I've found it to be soul nourishing and a good accountability of my consistency in Bible reading. The plan I use is on Ligonier's website.[72] Ligonier has a great variety of Bible reading plans and their TableTalk[73] devotional magazine is great too. We provide those devotionals for the members of our local church. If you do not have the habit of reading the Bible daily, start small. There are Bible reading plans that get you in the Scriptures for five minutes a day. Dedicating yourself to five minutes of daily Scripture reading is better than becoming overwhelmed with more involved reading plans, getting discouraged, and quitting. The point is to develop a routine that gets you in the Scriptures daily. I recommend starting in the New Testament and reading it through before beginning in the Old Testament. And as a word of encouragement if you miss a day do not fret. Also, don't worry about playing catch up in your reading plan. Every day you read, simply find the corresponding day

---

[72] www.ligonier.org/blog/bible-reading-plans.
[73] www.tabletalkmagazine.com.

Spiritual Disciplines

and pick up there. There is no need to be burdened by days or weeks of missed Bible readings that seem too daunting to catch up on. All that approach will do is paralyze and depress you even more. Read today's assigned reading.

Meditating on and memorizing the Word is also an important part of hiding God's Word in your heart (Ps. 119:11) and a very practical way to ensure you are digesting the Scriptures. I've already introduced and defined meditation for you in chapter 3, so I won't rehash that here. However, believers must grow to understand that meditating and memorizing the Scripture helps you internalize the Word, keeps your passion warm for Christ, and moves you toward being a doer of the Word and not just a hearer of the Word (Ja. 1:22). It requires what Donald Whitney calls "constructive mental activity."[74] The Lord will transform the interior life of a Christian devoted to thinking upon and memorizing his Word. Dallas Willard once said, "As a pastor, teacher, and counselor I have repeatedly seen the transformation of the inner and outer life that comes simply from memorization and meditation upon Scripture."[75] Meditating and memorizing Scripture is a powerful weapon in your fight against depression.

There are a couple of ways you can practice these two disciplines effectively. I recommend starting with memorization because I've found that memorizing Scripture is a good "on ramp" for meditating on the Scripture. I use an App called *The Bible Memory App* and it is available for Androids and iPhones (if you don't have a smart phone, or would rather not use one, good old fashion index cards will do). The app is a neat tool designed to help you memorize God's Word more effectively. You can create a list of verses, organize them by themed folders, and even invite

---

[74] Donald S. Whitney, *Spiritual Disciplines for the Christian Life* (Colorado Springs, CO: NavPress, 2014), 47.
[75] Dallas Willard, *The Spirit of the Disciplines: Understanding How God Changes Lives* (New York, NY: HarperOne, 1988), 150.

The Day of Trouble

friends and family to join you in the pursuit of verse memorization. There are also built-in reminders and re-visitation algorithms to ensure you retain more of what you memorize. The point is to develop a system that works for you to memorize God's Word. For our children, we use a curriculum edited by Tom Ascol called the Truth and Grace Memory books.[76] This allows us to help our kids memorize Scripture and particular doctrines in Scripture. This book series can be a great memorization tool for adults as well.

Memorizing can lead to meditation. However, more concentrated thought goes into meditating on a passage. When you meditate on Scripture you are allowing it to roll around in your head and heart over longer periods of time. You are squeezing all the devotional quality out of it. You are seeking to apply it to your life and work through possible implications as well. You are praying it back to the Lord. I think this is what the Scripture has in view when the Lord says (again) "eat this book." One of my close friends growing up was a boy named Chetan. Chetan immigrated from India to Southern Georgia (talk about culture shock) and he and I became close friends quickly when he came to the school I attended. As we got older, I realized that I *hated* sharing a meal with Chetan because he took so long to eat. He was convinced (and lectured me about it) that chewing each bite of food thirty times was good for your digestion, maximized nutrient absorption, and made you eat less. I later came to see the value in what Chetan was saying about eating slowly. Why he was concerned about that as a high-schooler I have no idea, but every time I meditate on the Scripture, I think of Chetan eating (don't worry, he ate with his mouth closed). Meditating is like chewing your food thirty times. You won't eat large portions of Scripture, but you

---

[76] Tom Ascol, *Truth and Grace Memory Books* (Cape Coral, FL: Founders Press, 2017).

Spiritual Disciplines

will maximize the passage's nutritional value for your soul. Memorize, then meditate on the Word.

These are all ways to center your daily life around God. As you internalize God's Word your perspective changes. Those caught in the fog of depression need help lifting their eyes above the fog. Believe me, I know this so well. It is so easy to spin your emotional and circumstantial tires in the mud. It is soul-sucking. It is fatiguing. And the tire spinning habits show us we serve a harsh master. We need our minds renewed. We need to look to the Lord. And the way in which we look to God and see our circumstances in a healthy, hopeful way is by committing and *submitting* ourselves to the Scripture. Pursue the Word-centered life—it is the only way to be God-centered.

Praying in the Wilderness
As seen in previous chapters, all of the psalmists struggling with depression *spoke* to God. They cried out to God in their desperation. This is our privilege in Christ Jesus who intercedes on our behalf (Rom. 8:34). We worship a God that hears our cries and groanings (1 John 5:14). We serve a Savior who can sympathize with our weaknesses (Heb. 4:15). And we have the Holy Spirit to help us pray (Rom. 8:26–27). Prayer is not only a privilege commanded by God, but it is a discipline that is genuinely good for us especially in dealing not only with spiritual concerns, but with depression and mental health.

I want to equip you with a few practical helps as you develop a right perspective and habit of prayer. First, select a location for extended, more concentrated times for prayer. Jesus frequently prayed in the wilderness, and he did so early or late depending on how you look at it (Luke 5:16). The point is you need a regular time and space of uninterrupted speaking *to* God. How else can you vocalize and cast your specific cares on him? Secondly, as you vocalize your depression use the Scriptures we've covered in this book. Which means make the prayers of the psalmists your prayers to God. As you work through various Scriptures and offer them as prayers to God, the Holy Spirit will be faithful to bring things of concern to your mind through God's Word that you may offer up specifically. Furthermore, praying the Scriptures allow you to see all the different ways believers approach God in faith. You will begin to develop prayers of adoration, thanksgiving, confession, intercession, and supplication. You will learn the rhythms, tones, and inflections of biblical prayer as you work through these ancient prayers preserved in God's book. Pray the Bible.

Next, I would challenge you to pay attention to the needs of others in your local church as you pray. Sufferers in Christ can sometimes focus on their own sufferings and fail to pray for brothers and sisters in the local church and around the world. Knowing of and praying for the sufferings of others put our suffering in its proper context. Praying for other sufferers helps you know you're not alone. It can keep you from despair, and it can build up your faith as you see dear brothers and sisters suffering in a way that honors the Lord. There is always someone out there suffering more than you. As you pray, know that God is weaving together even the worst sufferings against the evil one. The evil one, who is the Devil, wants to destroy you with your sufferings. God will use your suffering for your eternal good and the good of others. That is what he does. Just look to the cross of Christ to be reminded of how he uses evil to produce eternal good.

Finally, I'd encourage you to find a prayer partner. This is someone who will be committed to praying for you and you, for them. This person can hold you accountable to pray regularly. Your prayer partner can be your spouse or the one you text or call when the dark cloud of depression is hovering just above your head. They might not offer you counsel, but they will faithfully pray for you and remind you to pray. Having people in my life that pray specifically and regularly for me is a means God has used to comfort me in some of the darkest seasons of my life. I am eternally grateful to God for those who intercede for my family and me. No matter what, remember that prayer is a very tangible weapon in the fight with depression.

Repentance as Rest According to Thomas Watson
Now let's talk about repentance for a moment because in a book addressed to suffering saints in Christ who still wrestle with sin and live in a world affected by the fall repentance is always relevant and always needed. Repentance is the joy of a believer because repentance and faith are two sides of the same coin. Which means the joy in repentance is that it is at the same time a savoring of Jesus Christ. To repent is to turn in faith to Jesus. You can't have repentance without faith, and you can't have faith without repentance. And for believers this is a lifelong practice that *begins* by God's grace at conversion. Now for the depressed believer, the darkness can be paralyzing. In fact, in my counsel, I have found that many people caught in the waves of depression are so swept up in negative emotions that their lives are quite literally organized around it. Everything they do or don't do is in reaction to their depressed emotions. And because we are sufferers and sinners (meaning, we are complex), we need to understand that repentance is the way of rest. Because repentance is the road to Jesus who is rest (Matt. 11:28–30). But what does repentance look and feel like? This is an important question, because the quality of our repentance impacts our mental health.

Thomas Watson is a very helpful mentor on this subject. In his work, *The Doctrine of Repentance*, he gives readers six ingredients by which they can measure the quality of their repentance. It's worth using his hard work to evaluate your own repentance of sin. I will briefly give you the ingredients of genuine repentance Watson mentions. The first ingredient he gives is *sight for sin*. Watson

The Day of Trouble

states that "a man must first recognize and consider what his sin is, and know the plague of his heart before he can be duly humbled for it."[77] By "sight" Watson implies agreement. In order to see sin you must first agree that it is sin. So where do you go to see what sin is? The Word of God. And with an open Bible, you consider the state of your soul. I asked you this at the beginning of the chapter, but I'll ask it again—who is your master? Where do your habits say your allegiance is? What are you devoted to? What are you inwardly obsessing over? What aren't you doing that you should be doing? Are these things depressing you? As the Holy Spirit gives us eyes to see sin, we can begin to use biblical words to describe and address our sins. For instance, in my depressed state I may be neglecting the assembly of the saints (Heb. 10:25) which means I don't gather with the church. That is a sin of omission that I need to see as dishonoring to the Lord and bad for me. Seeing is step one. Or even paying attention to sinful *desires* that will have a devastating effect on your emotions if you don't see them as the Bible describes them soon. Having a "sight for sin" means I see sin as God sees sin so that I address sin as God tells me to address sin.

The second ingredient of true repentance is a *sorrow for sin*. Watson goes on to say, "A woman may as well expect to have a child without pangs as one can have repentance without sorrow ... he that can repent without sorrowing, suspect his repentance."[78] I have experienced and witnessed in others just how much sin can desensitize you. It makes you numb, cold, callous and cruel. It can make you withdrawn and embittered. Sin can have an overall dulling effect on your very view of sin. Even in our confessions, we hedge and make ourselves sound as good as possible. Or if we are confronted with the evidence of the devastation

---

[77] Thomas Watson, *The Doctrine of Repentance* (Edinburgh: Banner of Truth Trust, 2002), 18.
[78] Watson, *The Doctrine of Repentance*, 19

Spiritual Disciplines

our sin has caused, we listen to it stoically and offer a cheap, shallow apology—no sorrow, no remorse. Now I am not saying that tears equal repentance. Many unrepentant people cry, but we often do not feel the weight of our sin because we are so desensitized by it. If repentance is genuine, the sorrow will come because you are grieved by what your sin is—the highest of offense toward a good gracious God and against those created in his image.

Another ingredient of biblical repentance is *confession of sin*. I can't read Watson's remark without getting emotional because of how much I need to hear this. He says,

> In our confessions we tax ourselves with pride, infidelity, passion, so that when Satan, who is called "the accuser of the brethren," shall lay these things to our charge, God will say, "They have accused themselves already; therefore, Satan, thou art non-suited; thy accusations come too late."[79]

Paul says something similar, "Who shall bring any charge against God's elect? It is God who justifies" (Rom. 8:33). When we confess sins to God, we are agreeing with the Scripture about our condition, and we are declaring our need for Jesus. But there is also this sense in which we can rest assured in our confession that our sins were left in the empty tomb of Christ. That is what makes Satan's accusations "too late." Many depressed persons wrestle with their assurance of faith. They can believe the words of the Accuser because there is often much truth in what he says. But he continually leaves out the fixed reality that the King really does love us and that he gave his life for us and that he is near us.

Watson also speaks of *shame for sin*. He says, "Blushing is the color of virtue."[80] We are not a culture that gets embarrassed

---

[79] Watson, *The Doctrine of Repentance*, 28
[80] Watson, *The Doctrine of Repentance*, 32

The Day of Trouble

enough. In fact, I cannot think of anything that would be considered taboo in our society except for the mantra; Jesus is Lord. Blushing would do us some good. We have desensitized ourselves to the point that sin no longer makes us feel shame and the reason this is the case is because the vileness, comprehensiveness, and damning nature of sin has slipped off our radars. Our blushing over sin should drive us away from the sins we once warmly embraced and to the cross of Christ where "there is therefore now no condemnation" (Rom. 8:1–2).

In our repentance there also must be *hatred for sin*. Watson says "till sin be bitter, Christ cannot be sweet."[81] True repentance carries with it this Holy Spirit fueled hatred and disgust for sin. In fact, this is a sign of regeneration—of a new heart. Hatred for sin is a *gift* from God. And finally, there is a *turning from sin*. Watson describes this as a "perpetual fast"[82] from sin. It isn't that the Christian becomes sinless, but that his affections and loves change. Instead of finding pleasure in sin, he finds superior pleasure in Jesus Christ. This is the moment we recognize God's kindness in providing for us a great Savior in Christ Jesus. Romans 2:4 states, "Or do you presume on the riches of his kindness and forbearance and patience, not knowing that God's kindness is meant to lead you to repentance?" In our recognition of God's kindness, we commit ourselves to not trample on the precious grace of God but respond to our great salvation with obedience to the Word of God.

As we make repentance of sin a regular discipline, we also make resting in the finished work of Christ a regular discipline. Many people that struggle with depression would benefit tremendously from a biblical, robust view of repentance and faith. Everyone needs to cultivate repentance because to repent is to also *remember*. We need to remember that Jesus really is the author

---
[81] Watson, *The Doctrine of Repentance*, 36
[82] Watson, *The Doctrine of Repentance*, 41

Spiritual Disciplines

and finisher of our faith (Heb. 12:2). We need to remember that Christ is truly sufficient (Heb. 7:23–28). We need to remember that the Holy Spirit of God is the guarantor of our inheritance (Eph. 1:14). We need to remember in the darkest seasons of life, that God condescended to us in Christ to redeem us body and soul.

Conclusion

I've used the word habits/disciplines a lot in this chapter. The more counseling I've done as a pastor I've realized that everyone has habits; everyone is disciplined in some way. Many of us are disciplined in things that are not good for our souls. If you're reading this book it is because you know you need to develop *godly* habits because your habits can help reveal and shape your heart. But we must remember, that habits can only help you if you have a *new* heart. Good habits are nothing more than white washed tombs (Matt. 23:27–28) if the Holy Spirit of God hasn't given us a heart of flesh (Ezek. 36:26). So, with a new heart, cultivate habits in your life that center you on Jesus. Those of us who struggle with depression are often centered on our melancholy emotions, and while those emotions are real, and crushing, it is idolatry to center your life around them. So, dear struggling believer, don't waste another day on those things that drive you deeper into depression and despair. Cultivate habits of daily worship. Begin today. Read the Word. Memorize the Word. Meditate on the Word. Speak to God in prayer using the Word. And daily confess, repent, and rest in Jesus, your sufficient Savior.

Discuss and Apply
1. What habits (disciplines) have you cultivated over your life good and bad?
2. What habits should you stop?

3. What godly habits are the most difficult for you to cultivate and why?
4. What habits do you need to begin in your war against depression? Make a plan with an accountability partner and stick to it.

Chapter 7
Biological Helps

You may notice that this chapter on the body is shorter than the chapter on spiritual disciplines. That is because all people, no matter the circumstance, need to address the soul. Paul himself spoke of godliness as a greater value than bodily exercise (1 Tim. 4:8). But, do not mistake the brevity of this chapter as something to skip over or neglect. We must address our body too. Our soul is not trying to escape the prison that is our body. As mentioned earlier in the book, we are to be neither materialists (denying the soul) or Gnostics (by neglecting the body). The God who gave us souls, fashioned our bodies from ground and bone. Therefore, we shouldn't have a type of Gnostic approach to addressing depression. Adam's sin did impact our physiology, and that must be taken into account as we think through depression. Here is some good news: since God made us body and soul, he is also redeeming us in light of the resurrection of Christ—*body* and soul. Redemption in Christ is far reaching, as far as the curse is found. This means that the incarnation of Jesus (God the Son taking on frail human flesh)—his life, death, descent, and *bodily* resurrection touches matter and not just the spiritual. Christ added flesh permanently to his deity. He has a body. Jesus—truly man and truly God is making the earth (what is seen) new and not just heaven (what is unseen). This means that Jesus is making us new too, both our body and soul. Now, God cares about our bodies even now. If this were not the case, why would so much of his creation contain medicinal benefits?[83] We must therefore give

---

[83] See for example Abayomi Sofowora et al., "The Role and Place of Medicinal Plants in the Strategies for Disease Prevention," *African Journal Traditional Complementary Medicines* (August 12th, 2013): 210–220.

consideration to those resources that God, in his common grace, has gifted us with through which we can address our ailing bodies. Before I get into specifics, you should know that God has designed the body to want to heal itself. And while even that has been corrupted by original sin it is still a significant consideration as we think through addressing depression. And as a caveat, we will not receive glorified bodies until the return of Jesus. Do not expect a glorified body now. That is an over-realized eschatology. A new body is on the way, but it's not here yet. However, God has given us all sorts of biological helps to assist our bodies to do what they were originally designed to do and we should know about them and avail ourselves of them as needed. Now, here is the thesis of this section: everyone needs proper nutrition, exercise, and sleep and *some* people need medications. It is important to note that the medications I had in view at the beginning of this book are the ones I have in view now. On their best day, these medications seem to only address symptoms. However, I praise God for ways in which any suffering can be ethically alleviated. Nonetheless, we should always labor, so far as it depends on us, to aim to address root issues whether they be physical or spiritual.[84]

Nutrition
There seems to be a new diet trend every week. From the Ketogenic diet to the Raw Food diet, you can overwhelm yourself with all the information out there. I am, by far, no expert in nutrition, but I am a generalist and I encourage you to be one too because you are responsible before God to manage your health with his resources. This means that your health is a *stewardship* issue. If our lives are to be spent expanding God's Kingdom on earth as it

---

[84] I would commend two very helpful books that balance body and soul care well. The first is geared toward men: David Murray, *Reset: Living a Grace-Paced Life in a Burnout Culture* (Wheaton, IL: Crossway, 2017). The second is geared toward women: Shona Murray and David Murray, *Refresh: Embracing a Grace-Paced Life in a World of Endless Demands* (Wheaton, IL: Crossway, 2017).

Spiritual Disciplines

is in heaven, it's nice to do so healthy if the Lord allows. Many of us experience some symptoms of depression like downward mood swings, lack of energy and the like, and exasperate it by eating wrongly. Studies show different people process certain foods differently and we need a renewed mindfulness of things such as metabolisms and thyroid disorders,[85] as well as our family health history.[86] Working with a nutritionist that will consider your genetic makeup, daily habits, and family history can be a big step toward alleviating certain issues related to depression. In fact, blood work and nutrition could be the path toward curing your depression.

Your path toward healing could be your menu. Portion control is also a problematic aspect of nutrition, especially in American culture. Portion issues could be the causes of depression, or at least accelerators for it. For instance, some depressed persons overeat as a coping mechanism for depression and typically the foods abused most are fast foods, junk foods, and/or highly processed foods. Other depressed persons under-eat due to loss of appetite. This lack of eating produces all sorts of other health complications (e.g., headaches, fatigue, nausea, sleeplessness). If you are someone who overeats, under-eats, or eats poorly, be mindful of that unhealthy habit and work with a nutritionist to put a healthy diet plan in place. Also, seek out a biblical counselor to talk through biblical moderation.[87] Our unhealthy eating is a spiritual issue (Prov. 23:19–20) that has biological ramifications

---

[85] Edward T. Welch identifies other physical issues that can contribute to depression including Parkinson's disease, multiple sclerosis, lupus, hepatitis, electrolyte abnormalities from anorexia, blood pressure or even physical side effects from medications. Edward T. Welch *Blame it on the Brain: Distinguishing Chemical Imbalances, Brain Disorders, and Disobedience* (Philipsburg, NJ: P&R Publishing, 1998), 127.

[86] See for instance the research that asserts that no two people process foods the same including, twins: Sarah E. Berry et al., "Human Postprandial Responses to Food and Potential for Precision Nutrition," *Nature Medicine* 26, no. 6 (June 11, 2020): 964–973.

[87] Use, for example, the CCEF intake form: www.ccef.org/intake-form.

The Day of Trouble

(Eccl. 8:15; Matt. 15:36; 26:26). The way out is repentance, a spiritual feasting on Christ (John 6:56), and the development of better, healthier eating habits to the glory of God (1 Cor. 10:31).

In addition to your diet and before you consider medication with a medical professional, consider some of the supplements that your body may need due do a nutrient deficiency. It is vitally important to supply your body with the right nutrients so that it has its best shot at health and healing. Some people have reported positive changes by taking particular nutritional supplements regularly. Most of us aren't getting the daily recommended amount of various nutrients. If our body needs fuel to run properly, we should ensure we are giving it what it needs. So buying and taking high-quality supplements is a good step in the right direction. Omega 3 Fatty Acids, Folic Acid (Vitamin B9), Vitamin B12, Vitamin D, Chamomile, magnesium, and Ashwagandha root have demonstrated their value in helping to alleviate certain symptoms (and sometimes causes) of depression, and they are worth exploring in a fight against depression.[88] If you believe particular supplements are right for you, consult with a nutritionist or study up with all the resources that are available to you online before you

---

[88] Jay D Amsterdam et al., "Chamomile (Matricaria Recutita) May Provide Antidepressant Activity in Anxious, Depressed Humans: an Exploratory Study," *Altern Ther Health Med* 18, no. 5 (2012): 44–49; Mohammed T. Abou-Saleh and Alec Coppen, "Folic Acid and the Treatment of Depression," *Journal of Psychosomatic Research* 61, no. 3 (2006): 285–287; Mansoor D. Burhani and Mark M. Rasenick, "Fish Oil and Depression: The Skinny on Fats," *Journal of Integrative Neuroscience* 16, no. s1 (2017); Alec Coppen and Christina Bolander-Gouaille, "Treatment of Depression: Time to Consider Folic Acid and Vitamin B12," *Journal of Psychopharmacology* 19, no. 1 (2005): 59–65; MK Jayanthi et al., "Anti-Depressant Effects of Withania Somnifera Fat (Ashwagandha Ghrutha) Extract in Experimental Mice" *International Journal of Pharma and Bio Sciences* 3, no. 1 (2012): 33–42; Sue Penckofer et al., "Vitamin D and Depression: Where Is All the Sunshine?," *Issues in Mental Health Nursing* 31, no. 6 (2010): 385–393; Henrik Højgaard Rasmussen, Preben Bo Mortensen, and Ivan W. Jensen, "Depression and Magnesium Deficiency," *The International Journal of Psychiatry in Medicine* 19, no. 1 (1990): 57–63.

make the decision to take them. Again, your genetic makeup, diet, how you respond to certain supplements or medicines, and how they all interact need to be considered so that you can make the best, most responsible decision possible.

Exercise

Exercise. Everyone resolves to do it, but it seems we're all just too busy. Proper exercise should be routine in the lives of Christians and very few of us do it. While the Apostle Paul said godliness is of great value for here and eternity, he did not discount bodily training when he used it as an example—there is benefit to maintaining a proper, measured, physical routine (1 Tim. 4:8). A lack of exercise can be another contributor to depression and anxiety. In fact, I know many anxious and depressed Christians who manage their anxiety and depression by holding regular hours at the gym. These Christians have told me of the benefits they experience as their bodies sweat, detoxify, and circulate blood and oxygen. Christians should exercise in *some* capacity. I'm not saying you should join a CrossFit gym. I'm told I have the physique of Woody from *Toy Story*. However, I *do* think Christians should have consistent movement that increases heart rate, blood flow, and oxygen levels. I have a broken back and permanently broken tailbone that impair my abilities to do a lot of things. I know chronic pain really well. But despite my pain I move and stretch a lot because my job requires me to sit a lot. I try to get my heart rate up because I know it's good for me. I'm not a member of a gym, nor do I plan to become one at this stage in my life. However, I try to keep *moving*. Back in 2013 a PhD candidate at the time, George Mammen wrote an article in the *American Journal of Preventative Medicine* asserting that maintaining an exercise routine could prevent seasons of depression if practiced over a long period of time. He even goes as far as saying low-level exercise (20–30

The Day of Trouble

minutes daily) can have a helpful impact in the fight against depression.[89] Furthermore there are scientific studies that demonstrate a link between exercise and dopamine/serotonin release.[90] My point is simply this: fit exercise into your schedule. Don't bite off more than you can chew. It isn't about looking good, it is about your combatting depression with the tools God has given you so that you can be a productive citizen in his kingdom.

Sleep
Healthy sleep should also be a priority. A lack of or too much sleep is another contributing factor for depression. On average, people need between 7–9 hours of sleep to function well over a long period of time. Studies show women need more sleep than men and children need more sleep than men and women.[91] I have found that most people who wrestle with depression have poor sleep habits. People with bad sleep habits seem to flounder in life instead of flourish. Some people struggle with sleeplessness even though they are exhausted. They may seem as if they can fall asleep at any moment, but their exhaustion serves only as a reminder of their perpetual fatigue. Some people sleep too much (12+ hours daily) and are sluggish and miserable, and unproductive. Whether it's sleeplessness or oversleep a common denominator is bad nighttime habits. Every night looks different for the person who has an unhealthy relationship with sleep:

- No set bedtime
- No set morning routine

---

[89] George Mammen and Guy Faulkner, "Physical Activity and the Prevention of Depression," *American Journal of Preventive Medicine* 45, no. 5 (November 2013): 649–657.

[90] Saskia Heijnen et al., "Neuromodulation of Aerobic Exercise—A Review," *Frontiers in Psychology* 6 (January 7, 2016).

[91] Sarah A. Burgard and Jennifer A. Ailshire, "Gender and Time for Sleep among U.S. Adults," *American Sociological Review* 78, no. 1 (February 2013): 51–69.

Spiritual Disciplines

- Cell phones are on the nightstand and interrupt good sleep routines
- Too much T.V. before bed
- Eating and drinking too late into the evening
- Drinking too much caffeine during the day
- Failure to accomplish tasks that should have been accomplished already resulting in a list that keeps one up at night

All these and more can have a negative impact on getting a good night's sleep and proper sleep is a necessary weapon in the fight against depression. What you need is a routine that you stick to. Make a sleeping plan and stick to it. Do not under sleep (Ps. 3:5; 4:8). Do not oversleep (Prov. 6:10–11; 24:33). Sleep to the glory of God.

Medication

I recommend that medications be the last stop on your journey battling depression. Too often, we make it the first stop. However, because depression is not just spiritual, medication is sometimes needed. As I argued at the beginning of this book, we should be optimistic regarding the development of medications when those medications are developed to address actual issues. We have reason to praise God for medications that only alleviate suffering because suffering is pain and pain isn't good. Some root issues just can't be addressed until we receive our glorified bodies. Therefore, pursuing ethical, God-glorifying ways to alleviate suffering is a good, noble pursuit. Now, as it relates to medications such as antidepressants or anxiolytics, there is serious and legitimate debate on how the drugs work and their efficacy in peer reviewed medical journals.[92] Most anti-depressants seek to adjust the *monoamine neurotransmitter function* which is to say it targets the chemicals

---

[92] Erick Turner, et al. "Efficacy of Antidepressants," *BMJ (Clinical research ed.)* 336. 7643 (March 2008): 516–517.

in your body such as serotonin and catecholamines—dopamine, adrenaline, noradrenaline. How antidepressants interact or manipulate those chemicals is simply unknown. That is why some medical professionals are skeptical of them. Dr. Edward T. Welch, a biblical counselor with a Ph.D. in neuropsychology, says this about antidepressants: "There is no evidence that these drugs [antidepressants] treat a specific chemical deficiency that causes depression in people, but there is evidence that these drugs can change some depressive symptoms in some people."[93] This lack of evidence certainly warrants further investigation, but we should not discount the testimonies of individuals who have been helped with medication. We should be honest about what we don't know and be hopeful in God's common grace to man.

If you bear with me, I will give you a bird's eye view as to the chemical makeup of the body God has designed for you and as you'll see, you are fearfully and wonderfully made (Ps. 139:14). Let's begin with serotonin. The serotonin in your brain impacts your mood and even your memory. However, most of the serotonin in your body is found in your gut and is related to digestion.[94] Low serotonin alone is not a cause for depression; in fact, there is little to no evidence that suggests any single neurotransmitter sufficiently causing depression.[95] However, serotonin does seem to be essential to thinking, emotions, sleep, and food intake. Which is to say, your serotonin matters. Maintaining a healthy level of serotonin matters although we are not sure what constitutes a "healthy level" of serotonin.

---

[93] Edward T. Welch, *Blame it on the Brain: Distinguishing Chemical Imbalances, Brain Disorders, and Disobedience* (Philipsburg: P & R Publishing 1998), 125.

[94] Jessica M Yano, et al. "Indigenous bacteria from the gut microbiota regulate host serotonin biosynthesis." *Cell* 161.2 (April 2015): 264–276.

[95] See for example, Philip J Cowen and Michael Browning, "What has serotonin to do with depression?" *World psychiatry: Official Journal of the World Psychiatric Association (WPA)* 14.2 (June 2015): 158–160.

Spiritual Disciplines

Catecholamines are produced by your adrenal glands in response to stress (these hormones can be found in the brain and nerve tissues too). The catecholamines that are relevant to our discussion include adrenaline, noradrenaline, and dopamine. If it seems like your body is responding to something traumatic (people have called this the "fight or flight" response), it could be due to your body producing high levels of various catecholamines. This has been linked to headaches, high blood pressure, anxiety, panic attacks, chest pain, sweating—many symptoms that can be commonly associated with depression and/or anxiety. As I've said earlier in this book, I've also had physicians tell me that your body can have a sort of delayed "fight or flight" experience which could be why some panic attacks seem to come out of nowhere.

The theory behind various medications that seek to address depression is that these chemicals, if you will, need to be manipulated—perhaps aided and/or suppressed is a better way to say it. And while studies have shown these medications beating a placebo effect, scientifically we just don't know how effective they are. So, should you take them? That is the question you may be asking yourself and one that you wish I would answer for you. In reality, though, I don't know. This is where you must steward your own health. My recommendation would be to seek out advice from a trusted doctor (who isn't a pill dispensary). Furthermore, if this doctor knows little of the proper nutrition your body needs, seek out advice from a nutritionist. Together, they can help you discern what *your* body needs. Some people I know that are on anti-depressants think more clear-headed while on them and are thus able to receive biblical counsel. Other people I know did not have a good experience with them at all and needed to safely taper off.

If you do decide to take medication, remember that it is not your cure—it is not your deliverer. Your hope, your deliverer is

The Day of Trouble

the Triune God alone. And if you go down this route, also remember that medication isn't the only weapon you should have in your arsenal. There are other, more significant things to help you on your path of hope. But these particular medications may help address some of your suffering. That is their goal—the targeting of symptoms.

Now, I haven't even addressed other forms of psychoactive medications many of which are beyond the scope of this book. However, in the class of psychoactive medications we have not only antidepressants and anxiolytics, but also antiobessionals, antipsychotics, hypnotics, mood stabilizers, and psychostimulants. There is some overlap between some people struggling with depression and diagnoses such as schizophrenia, bi-polar disorder, and Tourette syndrome. I know godly people that take some of these medications too and some have shared with me that these medications have helped them. I've also seen people quit some of these drugs abruptly and spiral out of control. I bring these different categories of drugs up only to introduce you to them, so that you can do further research and have further conversations with your medical professional if needed. If you discern that you need to take a prescription medication, make sure you are informed on all the side-effects (both long term and short term). One study coming out of *The New England Journal of Medicine* that has been widely quoted in other scholarly journals analyzes the effectiveness, side effects, and even consistency in which patients with diagnosed schizophrenia take antipsychotics.[96] I mention that only to equip you with one (of many) peer reviewed medical journals

---

[96] Jeffrey A Lieberman, et al. "Effectiveness of antipsychotic drugs in patients with chronic schizophrenia." *The New England Journal of Medicine* 353.12 (September 2005): 1209–1223.

Spiritual Disciplines

on the effectiveness and risks of medications.[97] You must weigh the cost, especially as it relates to potential long-term side effects, and then make an informed decision. If you decide to take any sort of psychoactive medication pay attention to your thoughts, feelings, and emotions, communicating your experience with a trusted doctor—one who listens and preferably sees you as a person created in the image of God.

Conclusion

Just as we need healthy spiritual habits, we also need healthy *physical* habits. I've said this already in the book, but if God made you body and soul, to care for both then is an act of worship. Take personal responsibility for your health because you were bought with the precious blood of Christ (1 Cor. 6:9–10). Develop intentional healthy eating habits. Make exercise a priority. Sleep as unto the Lord. Generally speaking, you are not different than anyone else regarding your basic biological needs. Everyone needs to eat well. Everyone needs to exercise. Everyone needs to sleep well. Neglecting any of these can exasperate (or even be the cause of) your depression. And if you are concerned that your depression may need to be addressed with medication, schedule a meeting with your primary care physician and discuss how various medications may help you, but do it with your eyes *open*. Count the cost. And as a sign off here—if you seek out professional medical care, be sure to seek out a skilled biblical counselor to journey with you through your depression. A man or woman skilled in the Scriptures can be an immensely helpful resource to you as you work through and think biblically about your depression. So, pick

---

[97] I would also recommend reading this study that concludes that the benefits of antipsychotics outweigh the risk in chronic patients: Christopher U. Correll, et al. "What is the risk-benefit ratio of long-term antipsychotic treatment in people with schizophrenia?" *World Psychiatry: Official Journal of the World Psychiatric Association (WPA)* 17.2 (June 2018): 149–160.

The Day of Trouble

up your weapons, discouraged one, and use the means God has provided you to wage war on your depression.

Discuss and Apply
1. Which ditch do you fall into? Man is all body (materialist)? Or the body is a prison to be escaped from (Gnostic)?
2. How does the Bible actually describe you?
3. What are your eating habits? Do you eat healthy or unhealthy? Why or why not?
4. Does God expect you take personal responsibility for your health? Why or why not?
5. How much do you know about nutrition, supplements, and the like?
6. Do you exercise? If yes, what do you do and how often?
7. Do you currently take medication for your depression? Why or why not?

The Cure

I love stories that remind us that good triumphs over evil. A few years ago, I read Cormac McCarthy's post-apocalyptic novel *The Road*, a story about a man and his son after the world as we know it ends. The new world in McCarthy's book is a barren world filled with ash and cannibals and the struggle for survival. The book is quite colorless (not to mention nameless). It is gray and gritty. Even the format of the book plays into the struggle of the plot— it is chapter less and seems to be intentionally designed to be disorienting. Yet in the face of struggle, despair, and—at times—pure evil, the son in this story is concerned with good triumphing over evil. He believes good guys "carry the fire" and he checks in with his father throughout their journey to ensure they are still "the good guys"—that they are still carrying the fire. This post-apocalyptic novel won McCarthy a Pulitzer Prize and was well received by fans and critics alike. It is worth the hype, and I commend it to you.

    I think one of the draws of this novel is McCarthy's ability to demonstrate that good really does triumph. In McCarthy's novel, he taught us that the fire may seem like a flickering flame in the midst of all the darkness, but it doesn't die out. This is so impactful because this is the story of Christianity. G.K. Chesterton, in his book, *The Everlasting Man*, said, "Christendom has had a series of revolutions and in each one of them Christianity has died. Christianity has died many times and risen again; for it had a God who knew the way out of the grave."[98] In our struggle with depression, we yearn for good to triumph over evil. McCarthy's novel reminds me in many ways of the unique struggle with depression. Things

---

[98] G.K. Chesterton, *The Everlasting Man* (Moscow, ID: Canon Press, 2021), 273.

The Day of Trouble

seem colorless. The world feels barren figuratively speaking. And there is a real temptation to despair and give up. But all is not lost. Depression will ultimately be defeated.

We know that evil, which includes all suffering will be definitively done away with upon the return of Christ, when he destroys the last enemy—death (1 Cor. 15:26). And when we read a good book like McCarthy's novel, we cheer on the good guys and hope for the demise of evil ones because the story of good overcoming evil is the story we long for. When we get those happy endings in books, we experience what Tolkien coined as "eucatastrophe" which means good catastrophe. He explains, "in such stories when the sudden 'turn' comes we get a piercing glimpse of joy, and [our] heart's desire, that for a moment passes outside of the frame, rends indeed the very web of story, and let's a gleam come through."[99] Tolkien understood well that God designed us in such a way that we long for and find joy in the happy ending. Those struggling with depression long for the happy ending. And as we read a work of fiction like *The Road* we are teleported to a world where it seems like evil may have triumphed over good; however, in the midst of all the tragedy, there is a boy reminding us—to our delight!—that will not be the case. Then, we look up from the book and realize that we live in a world where it seems that evil may have triumphed over good, but then we remember there is an empty tomb that tells us this is not the case. You see, when we read books or watch films and yearn for everything to work out as it should, it is because the truest story is being preached to us through these very stories. These are all great stories, but they aren't original ones. These stories are telling the *Old Story* God has been narrating since the beginning of time. And this stirs something in us even as we struggle this side of eternity.

---

[99] J.R.R. Tolkien *On Fairy Stories,* ed. Verlyn Flieger and Douglas A. Anderson (New York, NY: HarperCollins Publishers, 2014), 61.

The Cure

All the bad stuff *will* be made right which includes our depression. God knows all, sees all, and all must give an account before him. Good will definitively triumph over evil because our resurrected Savior is returning and he has all authority in heaven, on earth, and under the earth (Phil. 2:10–11). There is a new, glorious, world made certain by our Savior who has all dominion. His rule and reign have no boundaries and the news of his kingdom is spreading to every nook and cranny of the earth and chasing off all remaining opposition. This new world is one with constant singing and dancing and feasting and drinking all as unto the Lord (1 Cor. 10:31). There is no such thing as gluttony in this kingdom. This is a world we were made for and get blurry glimpses of even now. And when this world is finally realized our depressed emotions will along with all of creation bow a knee to the universal Lordship of King Jesus (Phil. 2:9–12). There is no cold, harsh "always winter and never Christmas"[100] in this new world—it is not barren like McCarthy's world or ours (seemingly). It is a world where the flowers and trees are always in bloom swaying to the music of the spheres and where God's people can be warmed in the rays of God's glorious presence (Song of Sol. 2:10–13; Rev. 21:23). There's belly laughing and joy that is driven by our unhindered fellowship with our Triune God.

The Apostle John, while banished on an island, writes to churches facing immense suffering and committing various sins against the Lord and he speaks about that day. And in doing so he directs their gaze and ours toward something more poignant than our sufferings and sins and I find his words deeply comforting when I'm tempted to believe that I'll never be rid of this body of death (Rom. 7:4):

---

[100] This is how Mr. Tumnus describes what Narnia is like under the influence of the White Witch in C.S. Lewis, *The Lion, the Witch and the Wardrobe* (New York, NY: Scholastic, 1950), 19.

> Now I saw a new heaven and a new earth, for the first heaven and the first earth had passed away. Also there was no more sea. Then I, John, saw the holy city, New Jerusalem, coming down out of heaven from God, prepared as a bride adorned for her husband. And I heard a loud voice from heaven saying, "Behold, the tabernacle of God is with men, and He will dwell with them, and they shall be His people. God Himself will be with them and be their God. And God will wipe away every tear from their eyes; there shall be no more death, nor sorrow, nor crying. There shall be no more pain, for the former things have passed away." Then He who sat on the throne said, "Behold, I make all things new." And He said to me, "Write, for these words are true and faithful." (Rev. 21:1–5)

The words of King Jesus are "true and faithful." Though we may be weary from our battles, we must keep our eyes open to what God in Christ is doing in the midst of our struggle—in the midst of our depressed emotions. This new world— one which Christ instructs us to pray for with the words "Your kingdom come your will be done on earth as it is in heaven" (Matt. 6:10) is like a mustard seed that gradually grows into a large tree (Matt. 13:31–32). It is like leaven leavening the whole lump (Matt. 13:33). God's Kingdom is slowly growing and spreading and we need to remember that, especially on our dark days. For now, suffering and sin remains, but that will not always be the case. Yet, as we suffer and as we struggle with sin (Rom. 8:13) we can do so with biblical optimism. The Apostle Paul tells us to do that very thing in Romans 8:22–25,

> For we know that the whole creation groans and labors with birth pangs together until now. Not only *that*, but we also who have the firstfruits of the Spirit, even we ourselves groan within ourselves, eagerly waiting for the adoption, the redemption of our body. For we were saved in this hope,

but hope that is seen is not hope; for why does one still hope for what he sees? But if we hope for what we do not see, we eagerly wait for *it* with perseverance.

As we struggle, we can along with all creation groan for the day that this world finally wakes up and is brought to obedience in Christ (Matt 28:20). As we struggle this side of eternity, it is essential for us to remember that a world in which Christ rose from the dead cannot stay the same. It is impossible; therefore, we *must* hope. And that hope should change our perspective on everything. Just as Christ resurrected in this world, so will we one day (see 1 Cor. 15).

The New Jerusalem that John speaks of in Revelation 21 is God's Church—all those found in Christ Jesus. And the Lord has used sufferings like our depression to prepare us for that great day. So not only is heaven and earth new, but we are new. We are being made new (2 Cor. 5:17). We are the "bride adorned for her husband" (Rev. 21:2). Every difficult thing in our lives is leading up to that moment of consummation. And there are evidences and glimpses and reminders all around us pointing to that great wedding banquet being prepared even now (Matt. 22:2). Our Groom, the King is coming—*really* coming.

On this side of eternity where our emotions and feelings are riding this endless awful roller coaster, we must cling to the hope of the coming glorious, incorruptible, stable world. As we cling to the hope of Christ's return, our emotions will eventually catch up and submit to our husband, the ruler of heaven and earth. The day of trouble may not cease until this new world is finally realized, but the dawn is near, dear friend. Regardless of your emotions, wait in faith.

Now this new world is so much more than the dissipation of negative feelings and emotions. And I hope you've picked up on that clearly already. There is a critical piece of the new heavens and earth that we must be anchored to and I need to make it explicitly clear to you. I remember my wife reading a book which spoke of the new heavens and earth and this most important aspect of it was missing—the presence and glory of the Triune God. The anchor of our hope isn't the fact that our sin will be no more (though it will be no more). The anchor of our hope is not that our depression will be vanquished along with death (though that will be the case). The anchor of hope and the thing that makes the heavens and earth new is that our Triune God will be there with us and we will worship him for all eternity without any obstacles. As the Westminster shorter catechism says, "[We will] glorify God and enjoy him forever."[101] John uses the tabernacle language we examined earlier in this book here in Revelation 21. He says in verse 3, "Behold, the tabernacle of God is with men, and He will dwell with them, and they shall be His people. God Himself will be with them and be their God." In the new heavens and earth the Lord will tabernacle with us not just spiritually as he does now, but *physically*. Our faith will become sight. The Lord will be *with* his people. There is no greater comfort than this. And we will do what we were created to do—the only thing we will really *long* to do; sing, "Holy, holy, holy, Lord God Almighty, who was and is and is to come" (Rev. 4:8). As we do what we were created to do, our joy and pleasure will be in him as our light momentary afflictions fade to black (2 Cor. 4:17–18).

---

[101] *Westminster Shorter Catechism* Q.1.

Acknowledgments

Anyone who has written a book that has any chance of being good or helpful knows that it is a group effort. My wife, Brayden you have been such an encourager to me. You're my best friend and confidant. You've read multiple drafts and you've helped carve out time for me to write in the busyness of raising three wild and awesome boys and planting a church. Henry, Owen, and Ames you remind your mother and I daily of what is most important. I love you. Dad, you've modeled for me my entire life what it means to fear God and not despair. Scott Shearer and Ryan Davidson you talked through most of the concepts in this book with me and encouraged me to press on. Shaun Brown, you always asked me when this book was going to be published. I expect you to buy a lot of copies.

Chris Mouring, Armond Brown, and Kevin McKelvey you met late in the evening at a local coffee shop to read through an early draft and your thoughtful input made this book better. Ben Pearce, you helped me track down footnotes that I could not have otherwise found. Brian Hedges, your early revisions and edits radically shaped this book and somehow you did not laugh at my first draft. You genuinely taught this novice how to approach writing a book.

Jeremy W. Johnston, you meticulously combed through every chapter of this book and saw things I could not see. You spent much time with this project and you were so kind and encouraging with each chapter you e-mailed back to me for editing. Chance Faulkner and the team at Joshua Press, you saw the value in this book and were willing to work with me and never asked me how large my platform was. It is an honor to publish this book alongside of you.

The Lord has been endlessly gracious to me and has sustained me in dark, trying seasons of life. Lord, the dark really is like bright light to you (Ps. 139:12), and in your kindness you hold me close.

Scripture Index

Old Testament

Genesis
3:16 27
3:18 6
3:17–19 6
6:6 .... 71, 72
50:20 81
Exodus
3:14 81
16:3 43
32:10–14 71
33 44
40:34 38
Numbers
11:1 .... 50, 51, 71
23:19 .... 72, 74, 84
Deuteronomy
13:17 71
1 Samuel
13:14 41
30:6 1
2 Samuel
11:27 41
12:14 41
1 Chronicles
6:22–48 60
9:17–32 60
2 Chronicles
20:19 60
Job
1:11–12 54
2:5–6 54
2:9 53
42:2 54

Psalms
1:3 47
3:5 119
4:8 119
30:5 51
32 44
32:1 2
32:1–7 40
34:18 52
42 .... 61, 62
42:1–2 60
42:1–5 61
42:4 60
42:4–5 30
43 62
46:10 64
50:15 6
51:2 49
51:5 6
51:12 92
55:2 10
55:4 10
77:1–2 57
77:2 59
77:7–9 68
77:7–10 69
87:2 85
88:1 53
88:6–9 53
88:7 57
88:8 54
88:10–12 75
88:14 75
88:18 53

91 44
91:1–2 37
102:25–27 74
119 47
119:11 103
119:103 1
121:4 59
139:7–12 57
139:11–12 6
139:12 .... 100, 131
139:14 120
Proverbs
6:10–11 119
23:19–20 115
24:33 119
Ecclesiastes
3:4 76
8:15 116
Song of Songs
2:10-13 127

Isaiah
40:8 84
53:3 94
53:3–5 55
53:5 43
53:3–12 37
55:11 89
Jeremiah
15 47
18 81
Lamentations
3 44
3:1–18 33
3:25–26 2
Ezekiel
3 47
36:26 .... 6, 111
Malachi
3:6 .... 64, 73

New Testament

Matthew
  6:10 128
  11:28–30 ...... 43, 63, 88, 92, 107
  13:31–32 128
  13:33 128
  14:22–33 86
  15:36 116
  18:20 85
  20:1–16 51
  22:2 129
  23:27–28 111
  26:26 116
  26:26–29 93
  26:29 95
  26:39 55
  27:46 .... 55, 56
  28:20 129

Mark
  14:50 56

Luke
  5:16 105
  18:1–8 58

John
  1 44
  1:5 77
  1:14 .... 38, 56
  6:51–57 47
  6:56 116
  6:60–70 56
  7:37–39 47
  10:28–30 64
  19:28–30 94

Acts
  1:6–11 43

Romans
  2:4 110

  3:10–12 6
  5 38
  5:12 6
  5:12–21 6
  7:4 127
  8 .... 44, 60
  8:1–2 110
  8:13 128
  8:22–25 128
  8:26–27 105
  8:28–29 52
  8:33 109
  8:34 105
  8:35–39 36
  9:21 81
  11:35 51
  12:2 49

1 Corinthians
  6:9–10 123
  6:19 91
  10:5 97
  10:31 .... 116, 127
  15 129
  15:19 74
  15:20 43
  15:26 126

2 Corinthians
  4:17–18 130
  5:17 129
  12 44
  12:9 .... 38, 63

Galatians
  5:22–23 97

Ephesians
  1:7 59
  1:14 .... 59, 94, 111
  5:19 .... 62, 90

6:10 37
Philippians
   2:9–12 127
   2:10–11 127
   3:10 31
   4:79 7
   4:11–13 31
Colossians
   1:20 88
   2:2 85
   3:2 2
   3:3 93
   3:16 ....62, 85, 90, 91
1 Timothy
   4:8 ....113, 117
Hebrews
   1:3 ....92, 95
   3:12–14 70
   4:15 ....37, 52, 56, 97, 105
   5:7 55
   7:23–28 111
   10:25 108
   12:2 .... 55, 111
   12:28–29 51
   13:8 .... 74, 84

13:12–13 71
13:13 56
James
   1:2–25 98
   1:17 ....74, 84
   1:22 103
   2:14–26 99
   2:19 81
1 Peter
   5:6–7 92
1 John
   1:7 42
   1:9 42
   5:14 105
Revelation
   1:12–13 88
   4:8 130
   5:4 90
   10 47
   12:10 24
   20:11–15 100
   21:1–5 ....90, 128
   21:2 129
   21:8 6
   21:23 127

www.ingramcontent.com/pod-product-compliance
Lightning Source LLC
Chambersburg PA
CBHW050245120526
44590CB00016B/2218